This Book is the Property Of

Miss _____

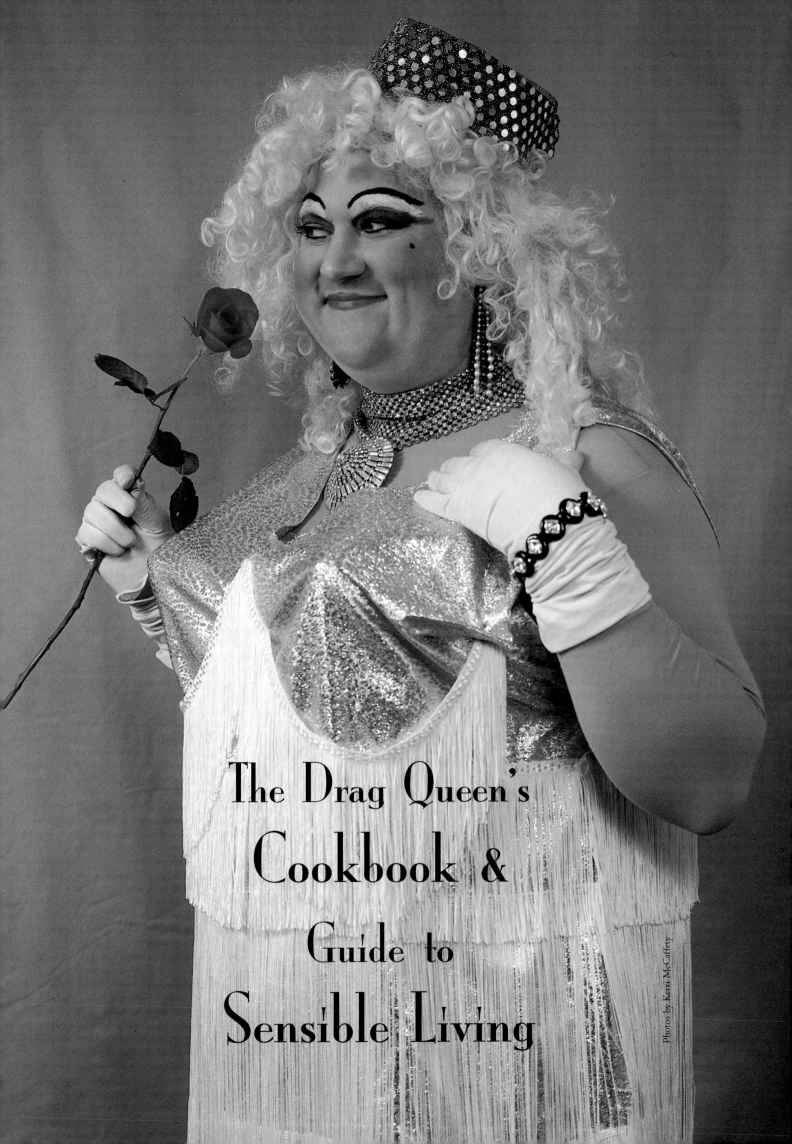

The Drag Queen's
Cookbook &
Guide to
Sensible Living

Photos by Kerri McCaffey

The Drag Queen's Cookbook & Guide to Sensible Living. Copyright © 1996 by Pontalba Press. Printed and bound in the United States of America. All rights reserved. No part of this book may be reproduced in any form or by any electronic or mechanical means including information storage and retrieval systems without permission in writing from the publisher, except by a reviewer, who may quote brief passages in a review. Published by Winter Books, an imprint of Pontalba Press, 4417 Dryades Street, New Orleans, Louisiana, 70115.

First Edition.

Library of Congress Cataloging-in-Publication Data

van Campe, Honey
   The Drag Queen's Cookbook & Guide to Sensible Living
   Includes index.
   ISBN 0-9653145-7-X
   1. Humor. 2. Self-Help. 3. Cookery, American.
II. Title.

Jacket Photos by Walter Thomson

Designed by Stephanie Stephens

When asked how this incredible project came to life, our Editor replied with a sly smile, "It was easy — all we did was giggle a lot and ask Drag Queens to take pictures." In our alternate universe, however, the truth is that this masterpiece is a result of the combined efforts of many truly wonderful people who were always willing to give their time and talents to Pontalba Press. Of course, none of this would have been remotely possible without the creative genius of the beautiful, talented, and delicious Honey van Campe herself.

Recognition must first go to our illustrious recipe contributors, whose willingness to share family secrets and their own individual tastes has now allowed all of America (and perhaps the world!) to savor "Drag Flavor." Unending thanks go to our models, whose astonishing beauty, abundant talent(s), and acute wit made every photo shoot an experience to be cherished for at least one lifetime. A multitude of merci beaucoups to our photographers, who gave form to our fantasy, and whose hard work and creative energies are seen in vivid full-color on nearly every page (don't deny it, y'all know you had fun!). Gratitude that cannot be expressed in mere words is owed to our "Director of Creativity," Stephanie, whose incredible vision and willingness to work *very, very* late brought together all of the diverse elements and made them one — the beautiful, humorous, and gentle world which every one of you, Honey's fans, are about to enter.

Lastly, thanks go to the families and friends of everyone who participated in any way, shape, and/or form. Thanks for your support, thanks for going out to the photo shoots, thanks for assisting with hair, make-up, and camera equipment, and thanks for allowing us to steal your loved-ones, even if was only for a brief time. We're just sorry it couldn't have been longer!

Pontalba Press

Photo by Rachel Greenberg

The Little General made it all happen.

Table of Contents

Arise, arise, maidens everywhere!

You have traveled great distances, yet there is still so much to learn.

What follows is information that I, Honey van Campe, have unearthed

from sources ranging from charm school primers to tête-à-têtes coast to coast.

Any women's book I found, especially those which were written in the years B.C. (Before Chanel), was often outdated and containing little relevance for the Transvestite of our age. They ramble on about a woman's place being near the hearth, and under the heading of health they seem to dwell for the most part on the topic of being regular. Well, today anyone, Drag Queen or otherwise, can tell you that the only satisfaction derived from being close to the hearth involves a chilled glass of wine and a hot date. And as for being regular, well, I always thought it more important to be fashionably late.

This is why the interviews I conducted were so much more useful in the long run. Information there was not only current, but based entirely on tried and true personal experiences, an insider's information bank, if you will.

Acquiring contributions for *The Drag Queen's Cookbook* was without doubt the most difficult task involved in its compilation. It seems our sisters are often less literate or sedentary than Hon had recognized (all the more reason for this book!) and getting them to sit and write a couple of ideas regarding their favorite foods was as troublesome as a Blue Law.

Of course, these gorgeous eyes do lots more than just prop up lashes, so I quickly recognized the nature of this problem. "Don't you just love these ladies!," I recall ranting to my girlfriend Sarah one day over tea and sympathy. "They tell me they can't wait for my book to come out, but then they don't care to contribute to it. Are they inconsistent or what!" At that moment a bulb so bright it nearly upstaged my usual halo went off over my head: the simple truth is, if they were consistent, they wouldn't be Drag Queens to begin with!

It was at this point that I really began to emphasize the personal interview approach. The information flow is more direct with such a method and the face-to-face encounter meant that I could also ask them to copy their favorite recipes down for me on the spot. You will notice as you read over the recipe section that they are all left as *sic* (or was it sick?) as possible in an effort to guard each gal's individual charms, i.e. to preserve the character of the characters who contributed them.

The other section of the book, the *Guide to Sensible Living*, presents the major themes which arose during my research. As is duly noted in places, it is by no stretch of the brastrap an exhaustive guide. Besides, as the world and the world of drag twirl onward, our lifestyle is changing at a heel-breaking pace, too.

There you are, my lovelies. Read on. Taste. Touch. Experience. Emote. Life is to be lived and what you're about to read is humbly offered as a symbolic first slap on the fanny.

Honey van Campe
New Orleans, 1996

*At last! At long last, the definitive words to live by —
a Beauty's Bible, a T.V.'s Tome, the Goddess-on-the-Go's
Guidebook! It's an exciting concept, I know,
finally having a proper reference for all those
unanswered questions and perplexing ponderances.*

The need for a Drag Queen's guidebook hardly requires justification. Just be still and think for a moment about how much a RG (real gal) goes through to look and act palatable; now imagine what a BM (born male) must endure and undertake to look and act like a palatable female! Any steps that can be saved, any conveniences and tips that can be shared, any way that our task at hand can be rendered less burdening must all be scattered to the winds like cheap pearls come unstrung. It is Honey's sincere hope that this book will lighten your load.*

This portion of the book is divided into three sections. The first section, called *General Drag*, is the most essential because it answers basic questions and provides a foundation on which any drag persona can construct and create. The next section is a brief discussion of *Household Drag* and offers pointers related to home decorating, housework, and entertaining guests. Finally, we peek into the ever-thrilling world of *Social Drag*, the plane on which we gals truly exist to make our marks.

The *Guide to Sensible Living* is an overview and therefore not intended to be all-containing. There are as many hints, opinions, and words of wisdom out there as there are Drag Queens — and these days that's a lot! This information is based on tips from hither and yon and is to be used in conjunction with the skills you've already learned. Read it, meditate on it, and apply the info to your own world as you see fit.

Always remember: You've traveled many streets to be who you are, occasionally lingering on their corners, and perhaps at times even lying in their gutters. You've invited the criticism and jealousy of those close to you. You've undergone the pains of razors and waxes in the furry depths of your nether regions. Gal, you really have paid the price, you've paid the toll to travel those streets. As you reach your destination, don't be shy about going out and being a woman all you want; it's not merely your right, but as you dump the pebbles from your slippers and straighten your heels, you'll know — it's also your duty!

*It is also Honey's sincere hope that your pearls are not cheap and are strongly strung..

The
Guide
to
Sensible
Living

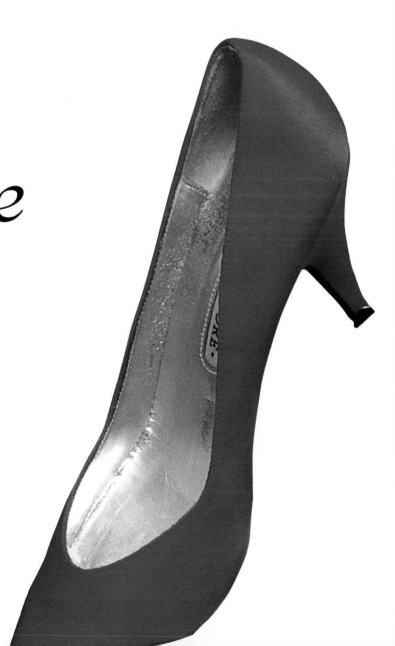

Photo by Lauri Flaquer

Call yourself these names.

GENERAL DRAG

*a*Rose is just a Rose, and a Rose by any other name would never stand out in a crowd. It takes a last name like Thorn or Complexion or By-the-dozen to get the masses to take note of you. And lest you forget, I'll remind you now: 79.9% of being a noteworthy figure is about seizing attention. Just imagine how different things would be if Jesus Christ had instead been named Lester Maguire and his mother the Blessed Virgin Beverly.

A Transvestite's name is typically as expressive as her appearance. Thought must go into it. It should be catchy, and it will usually be best remembered if it is witty. I have met the likes of Ginger Snapp and Polly Morfuss on only fleeting occasions, but their names ring in my ears forever like the afterbuzz from a handbag which has struck me upside the head during a lounge tussle.

As you consider your new career, nay your life, as a drag artist, sit down and compile a list of possible names. Place a mirror in front of you and one by one call yourself these names. *Immediately* toss out those which you can say with a straight face. One of the remaining names will stand out over the others and that, my dear, will be your own.

Good drag takes purseloads of effort.

Why are Transvestites referred to as 'Drag Queens,' you might wonder.

DRAGSPEAK

The drag maiden is normally witty and potent in the art of conversation, so there really isn't much that begs mention here. It helps if you are Southern, I have noticed, since ladies of the South are known for their spoken charms and clever expressions. If you feel lacking in talents of the tongue — verbal talents, I mean — I urge you to take a trip to New Orleans, where our wit and our words are as contagious as a social owee.

There are a few remedial expressions, however, that one can't help but wonder over. For instance, it has always struck my platinum head as strange that the word "Transvestite" is so often abbreviated as "T.V." Is there really an analogy to be made here with television? Granted, both Transvestites and televisions may be thought of as animated boxes that can change at the flick of their respective switches, and both can be entertaining to look at for hours on end. Perhaps, therefore, it is more than coincidence that they share this abbreviation.

For that matter, why are Transvestites referred to as "Drag Queens," you might wonder. Isn't "drag" a derogatory word with disagreeable connotations? All I can say to this is that you'd have to witness the sight of a Transvestite bringing herself home at 6:00 a.m. after a night out in stilettoes to understand that the "drag" adjective can be only too appropriate.

The Drag Queen's vocabulary is always peppered with endearing words such as "Honey," "Darling," and "Girlfriend." These, along with witty expressions, are accumulated over time and may be used even when endearment is not their objective. Example: "Look, darling (honey, dear, etc.), if you don't stop tossing your hair in front of my face, I'm going to rip it from your head and toss it out that window!"

Whenever a D.Q.* speaks, her patter should feature heavily accentuated verbs in order to achieve dramatic emphasis. Now, ladies, knowing your parts of speech is equally important to knowing the rest of your parts, so in case you were doing your nails in English class or diagramming dress patterns while Mrs. Barde was diagramming sentences on the blackboard, permit me to remind you what a verb is. A verb describes action — you know, when you do something or some one.

For instance:

"I *adore* your rhinestones, darling." ("adore" is the verb)

"If she *teased* her audience the way she *teases* her hair, her tips would
be much bigger." ("tease" and "teases" are the verbs to notice here)

Conversation is essential to being remembered, just like your name and wardrobe. The difference is that your name and your wardrobe make the first impressions; your conversational skills add to their impact.

Practice memorable conversation as often as possible, whether alone or at a Tupperware party. You should always be seeking new material from sources as varied as the works of Noel Coward or the words of Bette Davis.

*Normally, I don't like using the D.Q. abbreviation because I'm afraid someone will mistake it for a Dairy Queen, which is our specific name for a Transvestite with breast implants. But, my dears, I know you know better..

In drag it itsn't what you say that counts, it's HOW you say it.

ELEMENTARY DRAG

Good drag is neither cheap nor easy, even though Drag Queens are often both. Simply everything must be preplanned, tried on and retried, somehow circumvented, or strapped into place. Nonstandard ladies' accessories are typically required. Where to go? What to do? Is it worth it? So much to worry about...and this is just the starting-block stuff!

Then there is the charm and personality factor. Timing is key: can you blush on cue or lipsync Barbra, Judy, or Liza without rehearsing? Lots is expected of you — you are under the public's cruel magnifying glass the moment you step out the door, and sometimes even the minute you wake up each afternoon.

When should you go drag? Should you go drag to the supermarket? The dentist's office? Should you go to drag races in drag? Only you know what will be suitable for you. As you get into the Transvestite circuit, you will establish patterns and programs that are comfortable for you. Relax. Experiment. You have entered a beautiful new world that is only to be savored.

FAMILY MATTERS

Okay, you already dropped the big bomb on them a few years back when you left your wife and kids and the welding job. You dropped a whole carload of bombs when you finally told them that Michael shares more than just your studio apartment. How do you tell them about your fondness for female fashions without them feeling altogether like real estate in Dresden, circa 1945?

First of all, if you're going for the visual shock-them-and-get-it-over-with-right-away approach, at least dress tastefully. Recall the sections in this guidebook about making an impression on people through appearance...but just this once, forget about outrageousness. I recommend a smart skirt, blouse and jacket, and a close-cropped wig, unless they are Baptists, in which case the tresses should be longer, or unless they are Southern Baptists, in which case you are très bonkers for revealing any of this anyway.

If you're a sometimes Drag Queen, it may be easier to drop them a note telling that you're working as "a performer." This way your butt is covered if ever they stop by unexpectedly and your butt really is covered...say, with taffeta. "Oh, it's just part of my costume for work," you can tell them unflinchingly.

Of course, if their nonscheduled visit happens to be at nine o'clock on a Tuesday morning, you might have to embellish your story. Have no fear, though — anyone with enough imagination to be in taffeta at 9:00 a.m. on a Tuesday can certainly think of a good one to tell the open-mouthed relatives who have likely dropped the box of doughnuts they brought you all over your plush-fibre shag carpet.

Or, seize the opportunity. Sit them down over a fresh pot of coffee and whatever glazed crumbs you can salvage from the rug and tell them as gently and lovingly as possible that not only have you abandoned your wife, kids, and the welding job to open a beauty parlor, you're also a Transvestite. Hairdresser, Crossdresser — it sounds so closely related, anyhow. I'm just positive that if you say it with enthusiasm and joy in your smile they'll understand everything and congratulate you on your choice.

If they don't congratulate you and start to yell things like, "OH MY GOD! OH MY GOD! WHAT NEXT! WHAT NEXT!," you have little recourse but to sob. It's your only hope at this point. The louder you wail the sooner they will leave to digest the doughnut morsels and your earth-shattering news, driving homeward into the still-rising sun and vowing never to drop in unexpectedly again.

Subsequently, you might not be invited to your niece's confirmation or your cousin Bert's wedding, but instead of lamenting, think of all the money you'd have spent on icky gifts that you can now use to buy faboo new outfits!

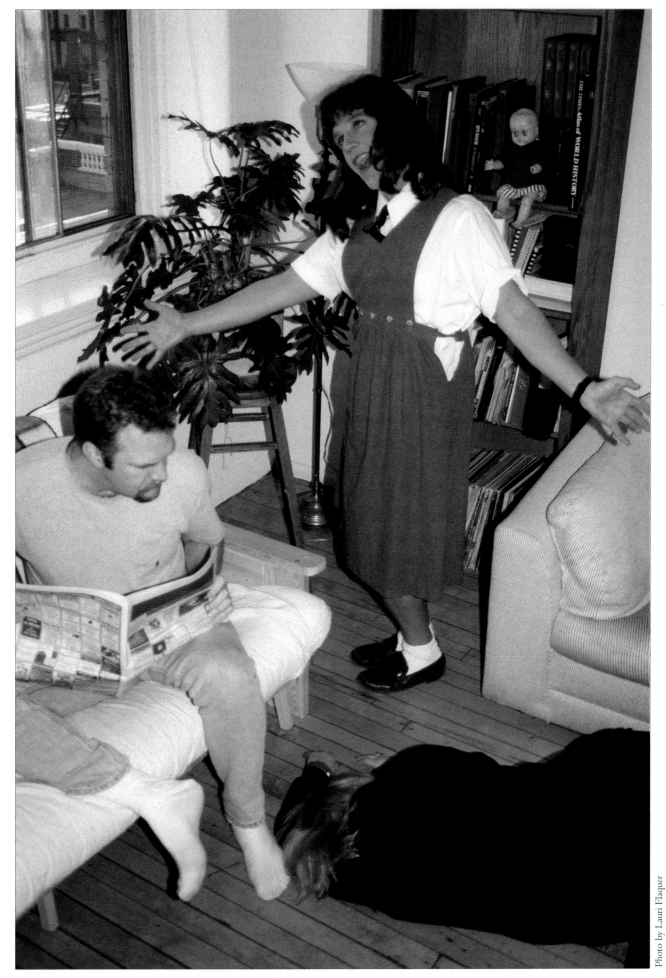

The Annunciation of Bunni.

LET'S ALL SAY GRACE

All right, sisters, this is going to be a tough one and, frankly, there's not much I can write that will change you here. Just always do your best to look poised and graceful, particularly whenever on stage. (I believe the stage is *so* desirable to a Drag Queen because it is a magic mirror for her and her spectators. She steps onto it, the crowd sees beyond the middle-aged man with multiple-chins who is wearing a gown, has unauthorized body hair, too much make-up, and a wig. As if enchanted by a fairy's spell, what they see is a 20-year-old beauty, a fragrant flower before them who is in bloom, and in pumps.)

A big part of being successful as a T.V. is the act. How can a strapping 200 pound case of terminal testosterone be poised and graceful? You act poised and graceful, silly! You pretend it and POOF!, you are it, my darlings. This is the magic of the drag fantasy.

It helps to practice and to work towards unleashing your charms. Try the book-on-the-noggin walk, for example. Use Crazy Glue to adhere some type of wedge between your pinky and third finger until you can keep it that way unassisted (about a week or so, or until the Crazy Glue wears off). Rate yourself critically as you perform into a mirror a number of gestures ranging from flirtatious giggles to fiddle-dee-dee wags of the wrist.

Perfection is so crucial to Drag Queen's success stories. You are an artist, an actress, a walking dramatic reference. Be critical of yourself because others sure will be. Know what is charming and makes you palatable, as well as what is vulgar and might make you appear vomit-esque.

We will be offering a more in-depth look at social skills later on, but for the moment, let us conclude on the subject of grace with this thought: For the sake of impression, whatever you do, **don't** be yourself! This should be a cinch in the long run, since not being yourself is the whole definition of drag anyway!

SCHMATTE TALK

Wear what you will, I always say. It is as simple as that. You already know how to select your wardrobe according to your own tastes, whether they be uptown sosha-lite or the naughty nun look of recent years.

I do think it's fun to put lots of work into outfits that will be seen by many. If you're going to a Christmas party, why not wear giant ball tree ornament earrings? An old acquaintance, Lotta Mulatta, once came to Easter tea wearing a bonnet sporting live bunnies inside chicken wire. She was the subject of accolades for many months. You get the picture – theme garb is a gas and the more effort you put into it, the more you will stand out.

Remember, my pets, clothing is a uniform which indicates to viewers – or in your case ogglers – the exact social category one is placed in. And if clothing is our uniform, it should only be fitting that jewelry makes up the medals that we pin onto the uniform with pride. The more flashes of metal a gal sports, the more battles she's probably fought, I always say.

Tremendous experimentation in the science of dress-up may be needed before you establish a look that is appropriate. Ignore the fashion mag columnists who say you should seek a look that is "you." Remember, a Transvestite is a Transvestite because she's borrowing somebody else's look! Besides, one of the joys of living in our technological age is that you can shift gears, being a sultry brunette harlot at a Friday night mixer and a perky blond teen queen at a roller rink party the next night.

Please use good sense in choosing drag outfits and accessories.

DO look over the following elementary suggestions which will set you trotting up the proper path of dynamic dress-up:

1. Brassieres (or as Bob Hope might call them, tanks for the mammaries) are frequently overlooked by drag girls because they are, after all, not serving any enforced public needs. I think a bra is a sign of the wearer's seriousness and it intimates a certain depth to her drag. A bra that bites in under the arm, or across the back, or whose straps are always falling down at the shoulders is a happy testament to your efforts to be authentic. And, hell, why not make it functional — stuff it with party throws or even bits of candy wrapped in perfumed pieces of paper on which you've written your phone number.

2. Try to avoid pocketbooks whenever you can. They look decidedly dwarfed next to your presumably larger features. (You know, one of you could make a veritable fortune designing tool-box-size purses for your fellow D.Q.'s!).

3. If you haven't gotten around to piercing the earlobes and you want to wear heavy earrings, beware! They will fall off and break every time you sneeze or titter on your heels if you don't glue them into place with eyelash glue.

4. As most of you already know, flesh-colored panty hose under fishnets will conceal the imperfections of your manly legs (i.e. fur) and make you feel trim, trim, trim.

5. Speaking of hose, never wear open-toe shoes unless you're wearing sandal-foot hose underneath. (It's all so complicated, just for a day at the shore — this is why so many of us prefer to grow hefty and wear floor-length caftans.)

6. To make dresses fit your upper area, cut the backs down to the waist and put pretty, stretchy straps across the back. This presumes that you are handy with a needle, thread, scissors, and spool. If you aren't, it may be a sign to reconsider your sisterly affiliations which assume a willingness to sing like a slave onstage and to slave over a Singer at home.

7. One of my contributors says that, for effect, you should paint "La Slut" onto jackets, blouses, or skirts, or even have it embroidered onto your tisket-a-tasket hankies. This will attract the attention of suitors.

8. There will be no jockey shorts on any of Honey's girls! You must decide from the outset if you are going to be fish or truly foul!

9. Hip pads are indispensable for a girlish figure. Just strap them into place, kind of like saddle bags, and build around them.

ACCESSORIZE THE POSITIVE

Accessories are oftentimes the **only** discernible surface distinction between a Transvestite and a Halloween reveler. Accessories prove that we are smart and that we take our drag seriously. Trinkets and do-dads and baubles (oh my!) represent how much effort has been put into an outfit and in my mind's eye, accessories are therefore the most accurate way to measure a made-up maiden's authenticity.

Part of your job as a drag gal is to always be on the lookout for accessories – to beg, borrow and...well, to borrow a lot. Sharing and borrowing is a T.V.'s way of constantly rotating her stock. You know – of always having an updated accessory collection without having to buy much.

BEAUTY ISN'T ALWAYS PRETTY

It's staggering what a girl has to go through, the uncountable products she must buy, the precious hours she must devote, and the hellish pains she must endure just to have a great time looking like a natural beauty. All beauty elements – microcosms unto themselves – must be scrutinized and determined to be either "in-sync" or candidates for disposal in-sink.

In this section we shall look at the elements of beauty separately and consider what efforts are involved in improving each. Again, I'm not intending to be the final word, since there are sure as sugar as many different approaches to beauty as there are shades of lipstick out there. Honey just wants to give you some starting points for that major task of making yourself pretty.

WISE BEYOND HER EARS

Let us start at the root of it all. Yes, your hair. Tresses are a **serious** matter, as they frame your face, which you already know, and because they can shift a situation from dramatic to traumatic with one false move. They can even initiate the drama in an otherwise tepid, lackluster moment. "Les cheveux font la femme," are words I'm often heard to utter in my sleep.

Which should you use, the God-given variety or the Eva Gabor-given variety? Well, you have tampered with everything else that God gave you, so it's perfectly justifiable borrowing from Eva, who, I might add, made hair for nearly as long as God. But if you really want to live the drag adventure as thoroughly as possible and use your own, I suggest you reserve a good two hours a day for your hair experience. No matter how much you love your hair, dears, I think you'll agree that it has treated you better than you've treated it in the long run.

Why not beat an egg for your hair? You know, a cholesterol treatment. This is a great weekly activity and it works well with a milk bath — which you'll read more about later. Just don't make the same mistake as poor Miss Mary Ann Wobbly who did the egg treatment and milk bath while still wearing her pancake make-up. It seems she dozed off beneath the warm lights of her bathroom and dreamed she had a whole cake on her face! In this far too real nightmare it took two friends and a can of PAM to get the thing off of her, and after waking up, and she looked crumby for days.

Massage the stiffly-beaten egg goo into your clean, moistened (but not dripping wet) hair and leave it for 20-30 minutes. Rinse ever so gently with water or brush it out with a wet brush. A Chernobyl breeze could not give your hair a better glow once it dries!

Be especially wary of shampoos if you are still hell-bent on showing off your own luscious locks. Some commercial products have so much detergent in them that they'd be better suited for washing you car ("LaVenus, why does your Mustang always have such a wonderful herbal smell to it?"). Choose carefully, remembering that your hair is just as delicate and fragile as you are.

The real story with hair, Honey maintains, is that wigs are invariably more convenient. And as their locks are stretched and sprayed to unnatural heights, those faceless Styrofoam wigstands do not scream and curse like a girl whose falsies have just exploded. Wigs are portable — they can be mailed ahead or be returned home long after you have. Wigs add merriment to any story when they turn up in the bottom of a punch bowl after a really good party. Wigs are so wonderful that our American founders (who wore the powdered kind) even named a political party after them.

While on our follicle fieldtrip here, we must take a moment to mention the unsavory side of hair in a Drag Queen's world. You hate to hear of it, I know, poor dears, but the dreaded reminder must be included here or I just wouldn't be fulfilling my duties as an Angel of Enlightenment. This book is designed to be your secret best friend, so let's raise the issue, get it over with, and move on.

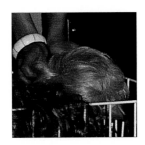

Miss Tomeka Kansas demonstrates basic wig maintenance.

Photo by Lauri Flaquer

Shaving. It's a necessary evil, unless, of course, you're on the advanced multiple-vitamin-with-iron-and-estrogen plan. Make the best of shaving and shave well. While doing so, say a prayer for your Mediterranean D.Q. sisters who indeed must shave twice daily in their never-ending battle to feel pretty. Lord bless their courageous souls when a low-cut gown is their evening fare!

Why not be creative, Honey says! You know the old saying, if life gives you lemons, make Tom Collinses! If you've got to smear and scrape the jowls and chin(s), why not add a few dabs of shaving cream higher up and sculpt those eyebrows? Instant face change! (Just be careful to remember, though, that long, sweeping Barbara of Seville strokes are fine for open spaces, but it's to be nothing but cautious staccato moves over the eyebrows. Your little lashes are already at a premium and you'll be yelling more than "TIMBER!" if you accidentally trim a row of them by mistake.)

If shaving is really a turnoff and you just can't reconcile it with the rest of your morning toilette, it's up to you to find a way to make it tolerable and, with luck, fun. Substitute whipped cream for shaving cream, for instance.

Lastly on this unpleasant topic, let us figuratively touch upon body hair in general. Ironic as it sounds, methinks you've really gotta have co-ho-nes to go out there in a one-piece ladies' swimsuit as some of you insist on doing. Those of you who do dare deserve extra points just for the grueling preparation work, most notably the mowing of the body lawns. Hair removal creams are the welcome weed remover of choice, although it still might come to using clippers for any stubborn quackgrass and thistles that have sprung up between the cracks.

If this is the case, give yourself an extra day between trimming the hedges and donning a one-piece Catalina number, since little red bumps tend to pop up where hair once thrived. Bustles and corsets notwithstanding, Victorian Drag Queens must've had an easy time of it, what with the high collars and full-length garments.

EXERCISING Y♀UR RIGHTS...AND LEFTS

Keeping your womanly figure is not a simple undertaking. On the contrary, great effort and time must be invested and a considerable commitment from you is in order.

If you choose to exercise at home you'll find that there are certain advantages, such as privacy. Use hat boxes stuffed with newspapers as weights. To increase weight, upgrade stuffing to cloth, then heavier cloth, and so on. And don't forget Jane Fonda (who one day soon might herself be resembling a Drag Queen) who is a great pal to have if you'll be working out in your home or trailer.

Health clubs are a bit more difficult for those who travel on our bus, if you know what I mean; they tend to be intimidating all around. I recommend arriving fully-dressed for the workout so that changing isn't a problem. I also suggest you ignore those whom I call "gym dandies" — they're the ones who wear matching shorts, shirts, and sneakers, and want you to see how much more weight they are lifting than you, but still speak in voices that could outdistance Yma Sumac's own ranges. These Miss Representors don't want you in their spotlight, so dash off and do some heel aerobics or something whenever you see them nearby.

Photo by Lauri Flaquer

Healthy skin from the bounties of nature.

SKIN IS THE WAGES OF DEATH

It's only consistent, I sup-hose, that a guidebook/cookbook should include health and beauty tips since what you put in your body and what you slap onto its exterior altogether determine who you are. Put your cigarette out and read on as Hon reveals a few of her favorite skin care secrets.

Firstly, I swear on my mother's G-string that vitamin E is the wonder drug of our beautiful world (and you ought to hear me swear like a seaman when I run out of the stuff!). This, accompanied by aloe, is as close as we've come to youth formulae; both should be treated with respect and be diluted or mixed with nothing more profane ever than, say, holy water or Brad Pitt's sweat (does he realize the money he could make?).

The "E" stands for energizing, effective, and en-vigorating, and this vitamin should be popped open and spread over your countenance once a week at least. Afterwards toss the remaining vitamin bead up past the gums and swallow hard. Leave the oil on for several minutes before rinsing off with warm water (or Brad-sweat).

Whenever I am out paying respects to my T.V. sistren I make it a point to peek into their boudoirs or toidy cabinets to count the skin care products containing aloe. This is the second skin miracle from nature and I always take it upon myself to congratulate the hostess who owns a sizable collection of aloe products. Anything from aloe facial masques to vinegar 'n aloe douches please Honey because it's all taken right out of Mama Naycher's generous womb. Use it in abundance and even grow your own! Got a blemish? Pluck a leaf off your aloe plant, peel it, and rub its sticky elixir all over yourself, watching that blemish take the first stagecoach out of town. Keep lots of aloe plants in your house or trailer – the bigger leaves even make superlative wigstands!

If you're already getting into an all-natural treatment mode, try my recipe for a simple facial. Apply a paste of oatmeal and milk with a little honey onto your face and throat, always avoiding the eye areas. The oatmeal draws out oils and barroom impurities that your skin has absorbed and the milk cleanses the skin thereafter. The honey makes it all taste good...once again, "Honey" and good taste in the same sentence.

And speaking of milk, there is nothing so soothing to *all* of your skin as a milk bath. Simply fill the tub with as much milk as you can afford and dilute with lukewarm wah-wah. Lie back, soaking it up for as long as your muscles are comfortable in a reclining position (some of you could be there til the milk curdles...).

Now that your skin is nice and soft, be extra careful what toners and astringents you use. *Never* are you to apply products containing alcohol onto your face. Trust me, alcohol's medicinal value is of interest only when it's taken internally.

Michelangelo didn't even *consider* painting a single drop onto the Sistine's ceiling until he was certain that the surface was smooth and free of faults. Like Mikey, you must take care never to apply your warpaint onto an icky surface whose cracks and crevices haven't yet been plastered. A clean face with a good foundation repels neither make-up nor onlookers.

MAKING UP IS HARD TO DO

A Drag Queen is by definition adept at painting on her make-up, so we needn't really dwell on this subject, except for a couple of practical pointers.

First off, be organized. Nothing – and she means NOTHING – is more aggravating than losing a small tube of this or a little cake of that. Remember that tackle box your granddad gave you for your 15th birthday? Bless his soul, it's time to dig it out of the basement and put it to some real use as your new make-up organizer! Keep your collection of colors in it, removing things only to put them in your purse for an evening out.

Always apply loose powder onto your face, notably over the nose and cheekbone regions, before putting on your regular make-up. This way, when you mess up the colors later on (and, if you're pretty much still a debutante you will mess up), it will all rub off without trauma.

Practice, practice, oh, please practice! It's the only hope that your make-up might someday transform you into something less than a tart and more than an android.

Once your make-up is in place for the evening, it is recommended by some experts that you spray your face lightly with hair spray. Think of it as a varnish applied onto a masterpiece to preserve it, particularly if you will be onstage or if you sweat lots anyhow. Should you eventually find yourself sleeping with open eyes and a frozen smile, I suggest you not press so hard on the spray button.

You already know that the eyes are windows onto the world and windows through which the world can peer into your soul. So be sure that the glass is clean by using good quality eye drops when needed. Be cautious, as well, in how you frame those windows in terms of consistent mascara thickness, carefully drawn eyeliner extensions (especially when they travel more than an inch beyond the eyes), and so on.

A beauty guide can't be complete if it neglects mentioning the paramount significance of dental care. There is nothing more indicative of a gutter goddess than a girl who devotes all of her income to gowns and baubles and none whatsoever to her gums and bicuspids. Beauty is only skin deep, it may be true, but don't forget, my tenuous vixens, that your beauty already exists by the skin of your teeth! So think of them as little pearls that you just want to polish the daylights out of after each meal, and see your dentist – professionally, socially, or any other way you can get him to peek into your oral landscape.

This concludes my beauty guide for seat-of-the-pants beauties!

Until they invent anything easier, a girl must simply abide by old-fashioned, step-by-step make-up methods.

Photo by Kerri McCaffety

Household drag abuse.

HOUSEHOLD DRAG

You know, a home is a girl's castle too, especially if that girl is a reigning queen who rules her turf with a forceful (yet feminine) hand. The home, both inside and out, should reflect her personality and particular sense of style as much as possible. A D.Q. is a public figure, a guaranteed celebrity in her community. Therefore, much attention will be directed towards her home.

The "don'ts" are few in running a drag household. For openers, don't ever mow your own lawn — it isn't becoming in the least. I don't care if finances reduce you to eating a stew of curlers, fake eyelashes, and wig clippings, you find an open-minded neighbor boy or a busboy from your favorite nightclub and let him do it. On the other hand, you are encouraged to plant, weed, and thin in your own garden, unless you live on a large farm, in which case hiring several farm hands is both necessary and something you might like to videotape!

Don't hang tell-tale laundry on the backyard clothesline if you have curious neighbors. Brassieres, bloomers, and nylons flapping in the afternoon breeze might stir up worries of reduced real estate values. As much as I don't adore the idea, a makeshift clothesline across the living room is still safer for your reputation and health, provided that the clothesline doesn't become a permanent part of your interior decor, serving only to decapitate, or worse, de-wig unsuspecting girlfriends.

The only other "don't" is almost a waste of ink to mention since it's practically impossible: Don't keep a messy, cluttered house! There's a fine line between eclectic/artistic and rodent nesting grounds. Dress pattern place mats and sharing a sofa with hat boxes is neither comfortable nor amusing after one time.

You must be organized at home! As your drag world blossoms and blooms, you'll be spending so little time at home that your housework must somehow be crammed into your hectic routine. Scrub the toilets or do the dishes (remember rubber gloves — those hand condoms will protect you every time) while you collect or spread your daily phone gossip. Think up one-liners you'll use at tonight's party as you clean the fridge. Set your hair and wear a bandanna à la Ethel Mertz while vacuuming.

Besides cleaning, your most important household chore is likely to be laundry. I advise Woolite for everything from wigs to evening gowns. Naturally, most of our frocks are of the beaded, somewhat intricate sort, and it can be real tough ironing around all those tchotchkied-up pieces. Please do so with patience and reverence. And, as previously mentioned, become intimate with needle and thread, so that you can both create fashions and repair them after strenuous scrubbings and even more strenuous wearings. (One friend, affectionately known as Miss Sew-and-Sew, makes a killing taking in alterations/repair cases from her less handy rivals.)

Go on and decorate your abode however you choose within the parameters of your own taste. Another sister, Edna St. Vincent de Paul, who once wasted a man with her bare hands simply because he wouldn't buy her a drink, returned home from "up the river" only to redecorate her bedroom in a prison motif. Reports came in that the cemented walls and metal bars here and there actually increased old Edna's popularity on the dating circuit, despite her prior reputation as a somewhat dangerous dame.

Just as we've relayed how important your personal appearance is in making an impression, the same must be emphasized about your home, my pigeons. Put cornucopious thought into it and traffic to and from your driveway will increase to the point that they'll be adding extra lanes!

THE GUEST IS THE ENEMY

The subject of visiting is noteworthy since social popularity is a Drag Queen's bread and butter. I once moved into an apartment complex and had the brilliant idea to go door-to-door with a bottle of Moet and a stack of cups to introduce myself to everybody. I learned that many people are embarrassed to have you into their homes because they just don't seem comfortable in them, or proud enough of them, perhaps. A few others, on the contrary, wasted no time inviting my 6'2" platinum-headed self inside.

You eventually learn whom in your circle you can just drop in on unexpectedly and whom you'll really best have a formal invitation to visit. People are funny that way, and I really think it's those who are disorganized and unprepared that make a big deal out of invitations.

So be it. In a sense they are correct: The guest is the enemy. This perspective means that the hostess realizes she and her home are under spotlight-style attack and that everything must be perfect. Guests inevitably rate you on their unofficial rating system, which can really discredit your social standing. Whether it's old army buddies unexpectedly in town or your best friend Candy at your door, you had better be ready to adjust the gladrags factor and the glitter element for whatever sort of evaluation a lurking enemy might have in store.

Dinner parties are quite the fashion again, especially since nightclub enthusiasm waxes and wanes and the streets are filled with those jealous upstarts who are just dying to mess up our hair. It's tremendous fun staying home and concocting a gastronomic production (look over the yummy and interesting recipe ideas in this book!). But remember our enemy rule and its corollary — dinner guests can be the worst critics of all.

It's usually best to keep dinner guests on a rigorous program, thereby limiting possible front-room whispering while you baste the goose in the kitchen. From cocktails to dessert to liqueurs and then to hell with them all is a good working formula.

If there's a slip-up and, for instance, dinner is delayed, give them something to stay occupied. That is, control the crowd. Once the weenies-in-blankets have run out but the roast is still crimson, yank out your collection of *Vogue* magazines for the guests to "ooh" and "aah" through. If the crowd gets restless after this and your microwave still isn't working fast enough, you will have to do something more drastic. Do the unthinkable — unleash them on a tour of your bedroom closet, giving them permission to try on, and, yes, even to borrow whatever they want. You'll never see your pretty things again and your wardrobe will look like the preacher's daughter after a Saturday night out, but the moment will be saved and no one will ever hate you for serving a tardy meal.

A smart hostess is watchful of her guests' every move.

Photo by Walter Thomson

35

PUFF AND MUFFY

Speaking of your home and your living situation as we are, there is one lingering topic before we move on: Drag Queen's seem to have a special affinity for housepets, whether from need of love and companionship or for the furs they might someday provide.

Choose your pet carefully! Cats and fish are quite all right, regardless of breed or species. Yet, when it comes to dogs, Hon is telling you right now that you'd better stick to the pint-sizes.

Big dogs jump on you and are likely to knock falsies askew. They often require unbecoming names like Butch or Killer. They require as well big leashes, bigger biceps on your part, and sensible heels when you take them out for a walk. NO Drag Queen should ever need big biceps or sensible heels. And as for Drag Queens using big leashes, well, allright, that depends on the outfit...

I've told you time and again that part of a Transvestite's never-ending journey is her quest to be noticed. Her look is very important, her house and pets are significant. The rest depends on the gal and how she behaves out there in that ever-spinning disco-ball known as the outside world.

Get gussied up girlinda. This capricious canine is ready for her strut.

SOCIAL
DRAG

Photo by Daddy Warped Pockets

The list of proper accouterments for Social Drag is longer than a ladies' room line after a coffee social.

FROM EMILY POST TO BED POSTS

Ooh, la, la!! Just look at yourself in the mirror – all dolled up, decked out, able to walk and talk, and possessing the proper home and family of pets. You're almost ready to be hurled outward to mingle with the multitudes in that endless parade of humanity known as the social world.

It is here that the Drag Queen shines. If she is to make her mark – something other than a scuffmark – it will be here. Out and about is where she lives to be and it is her behavior in the realm of the "out and about" which determines if our-lady-of-the-high-heels is to be a legend or just another stubble face. It is therefore mandatory that all of her social skills be polished like the finest of flatware.

Social behavior is a culmination of most everything we've already presented in this guidebook. It all overlaps at one point or another and very often you'll find yourself in situations where several sensible-living elements are in operation at once. Keep this in mind as you read onward about specific social settings and how to handle each one.

Emily Post really had the poop on propriety and most of what the old girl tells us applies even to your special circumstances. If you want to pursue the sister saccharine routine, you will need to brush up on etiquette. When you demonstrate a tactful ability to handle any social situation as though the graciousness goddess has waved her sparkly wand over you, friends will remember you and cite you as an example.

Let us provide some illustrations. In a crowd of people, if your brassiere becomes unfastened it is *not* good breeding to scream out, "SHIT! MY BRA JUST UNSNAPPED!." The respectable lady will softly state something to the effect of, "Merde is me – my cups runneth over," and excuse herself for repairs.

It is far too easy to succumb to vulgar means while talking of others. Granted, we all tend to be judgmental of one another and it often ends with cruel criticisms. As a fellow sister approaches your table in a nightclub, a gutter-mouthed gal might say, "What a holy terror that one is! Pure dog meat! Ha!." You can be equally to the point, but appear kinder on the surface by saying, "These tenebrous evening lights favor her."

I've mentioned already how much you are scrutinized whenever in drag. This really can't be emphasized enough. It is essential to your reputation that you use your head at all times for more than anchoring a wig. The resourceful girl doesn't lose her wits whether in conversation, or in any kind of social predicament. A sudden split hem, for instance, would never be a worry for the Transvestite who had the foresight to place a stapler in her handbag. When you chip a nail while out, do you put on a pouty mouth and go on home or do you know that a few discreet scrapes against the rough edge of a matchbook under the table will eliminate unsightly jagged nails and guarantee a long, happy night out? In other words, be prepared to wrestle with care any situation which develops. Tackle with tact.

Being social requires an intimacy with etiquette. Most etiquette is simple sensitivity to a situation at hand, as I've already demonstrated. But some things must be learned.

As an example, how many of you know how to make a proper introduction? This is especially important when presenting a D.Q. to a "street straight," who in his infinite innocence won't know if he should refer to your friend as "he" or "she." The take-charge, etiquette-correct lady will sense everyone's discomfort and make the following introduction: "Richard Normal, I'd like you to meet Gina Brooklynbrigida. She's an old friend of mine who..."

Do you see how simple etiquette can be? You get the point here, and so does Richard, who now understands that Gina is to be called "she."

There are loads of other things you can cram up your sleeves — even if you're wearing a sleeveless shift. Here are three wonderful, yet basic, situations, listed in increasing order of difficulty, which you should review whenever you want to make an impression.

I. *Sitting/Rising.* Try to do both with minimal "scoop." This will make you appear to be light as a hummingbird plume and help you avoid getting unladylike wedgies. Avoid putting your total weight on the chair arms and you will create the illusion of being nimble. Never spread your legs for balance while rising or lowering yourself; instead of pushing the legs outward, press them inward at the knee for weight-reinforcement and a feminine pose (bruises on the inner knees won't show up for hours, and then only if your dress is of a higher cut.). Those of you who, for whatever blessed reason, need assistance from others in sitting or rising should simply smile and try to come across as relaxed and as natural as possible. Grunting and loud moans while sitting or rising give away the matron who cannot control her body functions near or far.

Photo by Shawn "Doc" Murdoch

Richard Normal, I'd like you to meet Gina Brooklynbridgida...

2. *Ascending a staircase.* This can be tricky and necessitates great repetition before you get it right, but the dramatic rewards are innumerable. Once you've practiced you may graduate to walking from floor to floor with an air of determination and authenticity which will make people think you are important. The real secret to staircase mounting (not to be confused with banister mounting, which I don't invite even the most playful of Dragsters to participate in due to those residual anatomical considerations) is to point each foot slightly upward as you ascend so that the ball of the foot touches the step before the toe, eliminating a tell-tale clomp and stomp rhythm. Remember posture here – the railing is our friend – and posture's corollary, equilibrium, for whose sake it is best not to attempt the staircase feat after imbibing. If you've sampled amply from the bar and must use the stairs to reach the powder room, for instance, Honey suggests you bury yourself in a crowd of larger-than-life T.V.'s as they trudge up the stairs. Your only fear in doing so is that gravity might start to pull some of them backwards.

Before entering a room, pause to re-assess.

42

3. *Entering a party.* There are several forces at work here and you must truly be en guarde because you'll be making what I call a "mass impression." Listen outside the room until a new song is about to begin. If you can't enter alone, at least go in a few steps ahead of your party. But before entering, pause to re-assess. Quickly glance downward, going over Honey's three-part checklist which includes: the southern region (toes, feet, ankles, knees, hips), the middle states (waist up through chest), and the tundra (neck, fa-cha, hair, hat/headpiece). If there's no turmoil or trauma in any of your geography and you are certain that no flaws or undesirable bulges will present themselves, you are ready to open the door and step in.

Again, hasty actions are essential. Scan the room with military precision and quickly spot the person(s) who is your biggest fan. Lock your lips into what will be an omnipresent smile for the evening and swish your way over. As you head for the person, they will likely shriek upon seeing you. This is your cue to pose as everyone looks on. Have a second pose prepared for approaching someone new, and so on.

Be ready to work that room! Never stay too long — a common mistake that Drag Queens make is remaining at a function until the booze runs out or the houselights are turned up — but don't ever leave until three-fourths of the crowd adores you and the others are so jealous they won't sleep that night. Attention, attention, all on you. Helpful hints: It's often wise to send someone ahead to say good things about you, or, if necessary, to plant the shrieker in the crowd. Do try to use a different shrieker at each party.

Study the three maneuvers until you feel you have them down pat. Don't forget their common theme, which is to be aware of where your body parts are at any given moment. Particularly mind your feet, keeping them directly under you as much as possible lest their proportions draw admirer's eyes away from your real merits.

Not to worry, my pets. I won't go into an entire charm school course on social manners in this book — especially since I suspect that the paragraphs on poise and graciousness have already confused the bejeenies out of many of you. It's best if we just gather what we've learned and step onward.

LIGHTING A BIG ONE

It's important that those of us who smoke know the rules (allright, all of us know the dramatic value of a cigarette whether we're being Joan Crawford or our own wicked selves...which means that many of us do smoke like old toasters). There is probably no greater prop for our ongoing schtick than a good old fag. You know what I mean.

When to smoke, where to smoke, and most importantly, HOW to smoke. This is all really remedial drag stuff and if you can't get this part, consider packing the steamer trunks and hat boxes and moving on out, because the falsies and high-heels part is going to be even tougher to master!

The important thing to point out here is that you should always have a cigarette at easy access on your person, although this doesn't mean behind your ear — EVER! Dramatic moments won't wait, so just be prepared.

It also helps if you ambulate with impressive smoking accoutrements which serve to catch the roving public eyes and make them all adore you even more. Such items include an expensive cigarette case, a wonderfully suggestive cigarette holder, and a cigarette lighter they won't forget — say a strapping 21-year-old lad at your side who doesn't speak a word but is there to ignite your every smoke.

Get together with friends and practice the dramatic techniques of smoking.

GIRL'S NIGHT OUT

You have your gladrags to steal their attention, you've got poise to rise to their scrutiny, you've got your manners to win their admiration, and you've got cigarettes to get you through it all. Sounds like you are ready for a night out!

A telling observation can be made at this juncture regarding conduct in public places: everyday people generally believe you should never do anything to make yourself appear conspicuous, vulgar, or loud. A savvy Queen will do *anything* and *everything* to make herself conspicuous; vulgarity and loudness are just two of the many possible vehicles she can ride to get there!

The world has certainly changed during the last few decades and social opportunities for Transvestites are no longer confined to smoky bars and strolls along skid row before an audience of furtive motorists. Dining out with friends is an activity that's truly in vogue nowadays, particularly since it is such a great occasion for the T.V. to show off her collection of charms and manners.

Never be too relaxed while eating in the company of others! There's simply too much for you to watch out for. Table noises, for one thing, are a constant concern as they are really a nuisance. Don't ever eat loudly and always shun chomping or smacking of the lips. Drink with small swallows or sips — now here's a habit that frequently takes even the most willing of our flocks years of practice to master! Even noneating noises, such as the snapping of fingers or your trademark shriek must be curtailed until digestion is complete.

Your efforts to make dinner as pleasant as possible for co-diners means you'll be done and off dancing elsewhere that much sooner, so bear with them all. Don't distract them by making gestures with utensils or by staring at your reflection in them. Don't spill food — and if you do, be sure it hits the tablecloth, the floor, or even your neighbors, just not the borrowed gown you're crammed into.

Be tempting and coy, but do not toy with your food in a playful or suggestive manner — false eyelashes were invented to achieve such effects. Never comb, spray, or tease your tresses at the table, except when dinner is really dragging on and you're just dying to hurry up and go dancing. Just be prepared to go out dancing alone.

It is bad form to stash your dinner napkin or to collect those of the other dinner guests, no matter how many ideas you have for halter tops or minidresses. And while on the subject of napkins, only use them to dab at bits of food on the mouth or chin. You'll never be invited back once you've used a dinner napkin to remove crimson lipstick or to wipe sweat from your cleavage.

Common table etiquette is imperative even for the uncommon Transvestite.

Dancing is a terrific follow-up to a good meal and, once again, is a wonderful opportunity to show off. Just remember to follow your partner's lead on the floor and simply giggle carelessly whenever you make a wrong step. If you are with an escort, be sure to reserve the first and last dance of the evening for him. In between you may be the slut that you perhaps are and still be within the parameters of polite etiquette as long as you're back for that last dance.

In choosing a nightclub, it is desirable to have done your research in advance. If the venue is called "Ziggy's Place" or "Curlers and Cocktails" you're likely to have a good time within. But if your date is suggesting "Buddy's Bowl-'O-Mat" or a soiree at the local Elk's Lodge, you'd best be cautious.

Whenever there's an inkling of suspicion on your part, look over the parking lot as you pull in: 18-wheelers and pickup trucks spell misadventure, while Hondas and Mercedes foretell a gay old time for all. And, no matter how pretty you're feeling, don't automatically succumb to a "Ladies' Night" sign at just any old bar. Really, let's not push it.

Choosing a nightclub.

Photo by Rachel Greenberg

*Her frock will
surely be spotted afterwards.*

RESTROOM USE:
SOME FRIGHTENING PROSPECTS

There you are out with that special someone, all dressed up to the nines (and well beyond the size nines) and the inevitable happens. Your carefree evening is put into jeopardy when you realize that those 15 seabreezes have just gone right through you.

First, reflect for a quick moment, being grateful that you still possess masculine plumbing. It could be those extra few inches of storage space and that industrial capacity bladder that have allowed you to make it this far! Next, grab your pocketbook, try to blush, and excuse yourself from the table. If you're on a barstool, just spin halfway around and be sure your heels land squarely.

Hiking up an expensive gown while standing in front of a urinal is the sign of a poorly-bred gal. And, as if this isn't bad enough, that obligatory shake at the end of it all is likely to spot your frock from neckline to hem. Just imagine if you're in a silk dress – you'll be going home with permanent tell-tale, crotch-level water spots (admittedly, I don't know many T.V.'s who could afford a full-length silk number, so maybe that's just God's way of preventing messes!!!).

Most gay bars – and let's face it, girlfriends, that's where you'll usually be when you go out – will have nominal men's and ladies' restrooms. The ladies' rooms in such establishments are typically the best-kept secrets in the joint since most lesbian patrons prefer peeing behind their trucks out in the parking lot, and the few token open-minded and courageous straight girls who might've been dragged to the club by their gay worshippers are rarely open-minded and courageous enough to sit on the club's toilet seats. They'd rather simply remain at their table crosslegged, proving once and for all that real girls can in fact hold it when they really need to. The moral of the story here is that you can usually use the designated ladies' room in a gay club without incident and without waiting in line.

Notice how clean and sparkling it is in there. Seats are down. Nary a condom machine infringing on your sacred mirror surface space. Inside, remember the Drag Queen's formula for a successful restroom visit: PT/TP. That is, Primp Time (go ahead and crowd yourselves around those mirrors, they're free) and Toilet Paper (also free, and it could prevent you from having to carry your purse in front of you for the next hour).

The last thing I should remind you of here is that you are delicate, modest, and tender maidens, all of you. Don't ever spoil the image by leaving the stall door open while on a nature break!

DATING: WHEN TO TELL HIM/WHEN TO TELL ON HIM

Keeping her wits — and tits — about her.

Going out with gentlemen suitors is really nothing to twist your tiara over. However, since you've chosen this drag fantasy, it is imperative that you realize your responsibilities and limitations.

Always have him do things like open doors for you. I once sat in a cold Buick for 20 minutes before my date realized that I wasn't beside him and returned to perform his manly duty. It worked, though, and he didn't forget again. Similarly, there was never any discussion from that moment onward about who should pay the restaurant check, the cover charge at the nightclub we visited, or my cab fare home when his wife showed up unexpectedly. In one brief date that man learned many lessons.

Try to have the house prepared for a romantic evening just in case that Mr. Wonderful you might meet is sharing a hotel room with someone from his convention group. Your place should be vacuumed and generally free of unsightly glitter, sequins, and vacuum cleaner apparatus. In a word, the place should be immaculate — Lord knows you might have plenty of other things to apologize for later on when he reaches up your skirt!

A woman simply has to think of everything in advance. Champagne chilling on the side is splendid. Candles standing tall on tables and sideboards, dutifully awaiting ignition of their flames of passion. Musical accompaniment is set up and needs only the gentle touch of a button. Issues of *Honcho* and *Hunk* have been shoved under the couch.

UNION

Even though you do date from time to time, you might have written off ever again performing "The Act." Heavy petting by now is something you'd expect to carry on only with your poodle. What was once called your "thing" you might now refer to as your "relic," a resigned candidate for evolutionary extinction as far as you're concerned.

You will no doubt be surprised once you witness how much in demand you are! There will be dates, sure, but you could find yourself actually fending off suitors more than in your most unspeakable of dreams. More surprising still, many of them may be wanting to come home with you.

Out of everything we've discussed so far, and what with all the times I've reminded you about keeping your wits and tits about you, never has such advice been so crucial. Playing that female role so convincingly, you could easily forget yourself. As passions — and other things — rise to towering heights it's just too easy to let go, poising the heels heavenward as though they were tethered to happy kites. Your first natural inclination might be to thrust your groin in the general direction of your date's waiting knee. But first ask yourself — how well does he know you? I mean, does he really know EVERYTHING about you? If not, pause to fix him another drink.

If your date truly comprehends what he's in for and chooses to accept his mission, you must still be prudent and bear in mind a few points:

1. Never lose yourself entirely in "The Act." A D.Q. is always self-aware if she's to be convincing. You are a woman, you are respectable...somewhat...and you are wearing expensive clothing that stains.

2. I just know it was a practical-thinking Transvestite who first thought up the mirror over the bed design concept. But don't watch him in it — check yourself out! The greatest danger is that as your head lolls dreamily from side to side on a pillow, your wig will loosen its grip on your scalp, destroying the romance of the moment and whatever credibility you have maintained up to this point. If there's no mirror to monitor yourself in, assert your right as a woman of the nineties to be on top.

3. To a Drag Queen, safe sex can mean myriad things like keeping a blunt object under your pillow just in case his masculine perception feels betrayed by your anatomical revelations. But safe sex still means using a condom (don't confuse this word with "condiment" as my friend Cloreen did. Boy, was her date perplexed as she offered him something from a bedside relish tray!). You've managed to remember layer upon layer of frivolous garb for the evening; be prepared to put on this one very practical layer. If you find yourself in a pinch without condoms, a shower cap and rubber band may not be ideal, but it will get you through an otherwise sticky situation.

To some gals, safer sex means always keeping condiments at hand.

The final word on dating is that it's usually easiest if you can get rid of him before you actually retire for the night. The morning-after syndrome is generally awkward enough, but in your special case, both the passions and the liquor of the previous evening have worn off and you just don't want to risk instigating a murder/suicide event. If you do risk it and he stays the night, Honey warns you right now to leave your wig on and *do not* fall asleep under any conditions! You'll be shaky in the morning, but your face won't be rubbed off across the pillow.

You should understand fully that, as a Drag Queen, you do possess certain advantages when it comes to dating. If your dude becomes a dud and won't leave you alone, or if there's even a smidgen of abuse on his part, have your response prepared: "You know, I think I met your wife today at the supermarket. She's very sweet, you know, and we're going to take a yoga class together."

SOCIAL DUES/SOCIAL DON'TS ─────────

The subject of going out is an important one since "out" is where you'll get your exposure. As long as your comportment is original and within a safe nearness to propriety, you'll do just fine.

However, watch for jealousy from your competition. There will even be some who might challenge you to a physical confrontation on occasion. At this point, I urge you to use the "Would you like to step outside?" method. Once she has stepped outside, lock the bitch out if possible, or slip the bouncer a twenty and some specific instructions, and resume enjoying your evening indoors.

Dear ladies, just as there are situations to avoid, there are a few places which I blanketly place in my caveat column. Church is perhaps a wonderful idea for many but you might not feel very welcome there yourself. There is an automatic conflict with the priest's drag, which has, of course, been sanctioned by God. Yours, on the other hand, is just reeking of Satan. The bare essence of my rambling is: think before you go any old where in your regalia. We might consider ourselves an advanced civilization but, sadly, there are still many people out there who would harm someone who is prettier than they could ever be.

I recall walking toward a favorite watering hole one evening and being pelted with eggs by young hoo-has in a pickup truck. My first reaction, as I stood there with egg on my face, was a desire to run home and bury my head in the pillow. But after a moment's thought I decided to carry on with my evening as planned, leaving the yoke, shells, and white for all to see and ask me about. Somehow, I wore the scrambled mess with pride, raising the collective awareness as I did so. The story had a happy ending, you'll be glad to know, as several washings on the gentle cycle took the egg right out of my angora sweater.

This is an appropriate moment to bring up a topic which involves society in general. To get this far, you've demonstrated the fortitude of a mother lion and the resilience of trash that won't burn. Times are good for many of us, but we rarely take an opportunity to give something back to help others.

Imagine, for example, the faces of hospital patients glad to be alive as you, their Candystriper, awaken them for a meal. Your favorite political candidate won't know how to thank you for volunteering your services for his or her campaign. And what about expanding your own horizons by joining a nonprofit organization like the Daughters of the American Revolution or N.O.W.? How about organizing an old-fashioned quilting bee for charity? You see, the world can really be made into a better place through drag, not in spite of it, as many have wanted to believe over time.

DRAG OF THE FUTURE

Sweet Mother of Pearl! We really are everywhere nowadays, aren't we? It just seems that one cannot go to the bookstore, the cinema, or even stay home and watch reruns of "Lassie" without there being some drag elements which only a few piddly years ago would have been unthinkable. Drag has gone from being our secret to no secret at all.

Where will it all go from here one has to wonder. Honey has visions of drag merit badges in the scouts, drag sensitivity lessons in public schools (mainly just a bunch of makeovers and a bit of required reading on the life of Coco Chanel), and even a new approach to Sweet Sixteen Coming Out Parties. Could there be Dragstronauts in outer space? Drag in the White House?

While it's fun to picture things loftier than our own wig heights, let us never forget the nobility and respectability of common drag. "COMMON DRAG!," you shriek. "What an oxymoron!" Nay, nay sayeth Honey. We must never forget the significance of everyday Transvestites who simply exist in their own splendor of lamé and sequin-bedecked trailers. You see, despite the requisite gowns and accessories, drag is not just a tangible, material achievement at all. It is a state of mind which is attained only after arduous years of teasing, stuffing and tugging — a nirvana of sorts. The end of the lovely road.

Go out now and live the drag fantasy. Think of yourself in the proper light: you aren't a teacher, you're a Professora; you aren't a waitperson, you're a Diner Diva; you aren't a flight attendant, you're a Heavenly Hostess; you aren't even an unemployed person, you're an Oprah Engineer! Why even think of yourself as just a grown-up when you can be an Adultress! The key to happy, successful drag, it is revealed here, is how you perceive yourself *before* you present yourself. No truer advice can be told, no greater gift can I offer you than this.

With tears of joy and pride in her eyes, and a few broken nails, Honey must stop for now. Out into the universe you go as Ambassadresses-In-Dresses, remembering well what I have taught you: be charming, be elegant, be noticed. You are all, everyone of you, fabulous and beautiful already.

The
Drag
Queen's
Cookbook

It's time to get down and get cooking!

SOME INTRODUCTORY THOUGHTS

It's time to get down and get cooking! You're about to encounter Honey's collection of recipes ranging from the basic to the unusual, all donated by Transvestites who themselves range from the unusual to the unusual. The recipes resemble their suppliers in another way: most of them are unlikely mixtures of disparate ingredients – just like a Drag Queen!

First, though, some handy ideas on food and cooking. You, as a Drag Queen, should be creative with food just as you would be with make-up and accessories. Take a simple egg as an example, considering some of its various legal uses: egg salad with curry and tomatoes, artichoke and cheddar omelets, hard-cooked egg on cucumber slices (yes, dears, cucumbers are edible too) with a few drops of salad dressing, eggs with their guts blown out and then dyed to make Easter earrings, egg hair treatment (hope you read the "Beauty Isn't Always Pretty" section) and so on down the old conveyer belt of ideas. A little ingenuity and a few eggs can make for a whole lot of fun.

Some foods, like our friend the egg, are multifunctional. An avocado is a great example – it's as satisfying in an avocado daiquiri (toss ice, sugar, lemon juice, and avocado chunks into the blender) as it is on your skin as a facial cream (mash and spread over skin). In fact, a good rule of thumb is that if you can make daiquiris with something, chances are it will also make a tip-top facial compound.

The nutrition-minded gal should refer back to the Drag Queen's Basic Four Food Groups — Hors d'Oeuvres, Drinks, Stuff You Eat, and Fish. Recipes for each of these categories are provided, except for Fish, which has been left out for reasons well-known to any card-carrying Drag Gal.

Hors d' Oeuvres are a key staple because it's often that friends — or others — will drop over after a performance or a special night out ("drop" is an appropriate word choice since it is usually as though they've crashed right through the ceiling, landing in your furniture where they stay stuck for hours).

Under their teased wigs lurk man-sized appetites demanding satiation. The ill-prepared girl suddenly finds herself as blank as a cow watching the trains go by as she stands there all alone in her kitchen. The ever-ready hostess will have snacks pre-arranged on serving dishes or cookie sheets, as the case may be, ready for microwave or broiler. The quick-thinking gal who hasn't prepared any treats in advance should be able to assemble something tasty and out-of-the-ordinary for her special guests in the brief time in takes them to deplete her liquor stock.

Bon-bons are normally a wise item to stock in your pantry. They're bite-size and delicious — two big criteria for proper hors d'oeuvres. Besides, they'll fill your friends up and ruin their girlish figures in no time flat!

NUTRITION THIS!

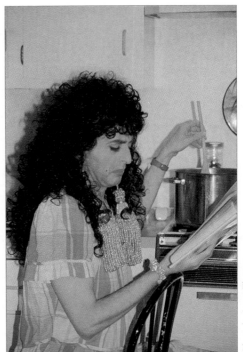

Photo by Lauri Flaquer

Making a meal with love — wrong.

Keep in mind that the more unusual the hors d'oeuvres the better. Those Queens will be talking about you later on anyhow, so why not provide the subject matter in the form of zingy meatballs-in-blankets or bite-size quiches?

Drinks are another weight-worthy member of the Basic Four Food Group club. You are what you drink, I always say. That is, whatever you order is a very significant reflection of who you are. If you holler, "One Fuzzy Navel" to a bartender, she just might try to check! Whiskey and gin are signs of jaded dames, and beer, even if served up in a pilsner glass, isn't very feminine. In fact, root beer floats should be about as masculine as your imbibing gets. If you can afford good champagne, it is tingly, sexy, and oh, so girlish.

Meats and veggies are the two main elements of the Stuff You Eat category. Most meats, however, should be avoided, especially red meats, which tend to be somewhat butch (what do you think put the "butch" in butcher?). On the other hand, keeping a steak in the freezer is handy for bruises and welts obtained during a lounge scuffle or after nearly being high-heeled to death during a last-call stampede.

Under no circumstances will the self-respecting T.V. be seen eating a frankfurter in public. This is vulgar and obvious! For the gal who craves her weenies, franks and beans might seem a safe alternative — after all, everything is so diminutive and nonthreatening. Still, it's reminiscent of campfire grub and if you must partake, do so when alone at home, shutters shut.

You know, vegetables are healthful and delicious, but it must be officially stated up front that they carry a heavy flatulence factor! Alas, imagine yourself on stage about to be judged in the Miss Big Hair Pageant of your county or parish, and you lose yourself in an uncontrolled and certainly unplanned medley of poo-poos. Minutes, perhaps hours, of preparation for the event would be for naught as your poise scores go into double-digit negative numbers. What's worse, think of how they'll all talk for weeks to come. "Oh, here comes Connie Cloudburst! Should've crowned that one Bean Queen! Tee hee, tittle tittle."

Making a meal with love — right.

Just remember this oft-unspoken, yet essential corollary of creating the drag illusion: you can cake colors on your face until the bovines are back and you can even go all the way under the chopping block to have a gender flip-flop, but you'll always possess a man's unpretty-odor-release glands. They are decidedly different from those of a (ahem!) real woman and, worse, they are entirely impossible to medically locate for removal. Yes, your beauty might take their breath away and your gowns might have them gasping, but they'll be downright suffocating if you don't accept this one fact of physiology and adjust your diet accordingly.

Therefore, a sincere Drag Queen has an easier time of it if she sticks to the Hors d' Oeuvres and Drinks categories as her basic sources of sustenance (watch for my own "Drag Queen's Diet" leaflet coming out with the upcoming "Drag Queen's Workout" aerobic video). Nevertheless, we've exposed you to food in general and now you're ready to start reading – and preparing – the savory recipes provided by fellow Transvestites from all over.

The omnipresent-of-mind Honster has taken it upon herself to organize all the contributed concoctions into meal themes. I have formulated everything so that you can devote longer moments to preparing yourself with appropriate attentions (my formula is dress/overdress/undress/redress) as the meals more or less prepare themselves. As you study, and, if my task has been accomplished properly, memorize the pages that follow and begin to plan your next food event. If the depth and details of my meal themes overwhelm you, practice first on inconsequential friends before actually culinating anything of importance for royalty. Remember to accessorize those meals, too: Drag Ladies don't do many favors, it is true, but we sure love to supply them at our fiestas!

Speaking of favors, Hon has also deemed it necessary to provide her faithful and gentle readers with a legend (don't fret, its not the one in my own mind) that provides translations to the dragified cooking measurements included in the tasty recipes. Here you go, my dears:

> bsp. = big spoon = tablespoon
> lsp. = little spoon = teaspoon
> wtf. = wrist flick = dash

Heels off, aprons in place, the moment has arrived to find your kitchen. Go ahead now, eat, drink, and be Marys!!

Photo by Lauri Flaquer

GALA DINNER FOR ONE

There you are, all dolled up with so much to do! With Ronda, Sara Lee, and Tizzy all miffed at you over that ridiculous misunderstanding at the thrift store (you still don't know how the thing got in your purse!) let them just sniff and pout all they want. You're planning a sumptuous supper for one, a feast so fabulous you won't even notice you're dining alone. When was the last time you spent any quality time with your favorite person, anyway?

The only rule to this menu is that you must make it in its entirety. "But what will I ever do with all that food?!?," you gasp. Well, I believe deep down in my pretty little pumper that Ronda, Sara Lee, and Tizzy will hear all the squeals of merriment coming from your dining table and figure out how much fun you're having all by your selfish self. By tomorrow evening they'll be glittering your doorstep once more, and when they do, punish them with leftovers!

COTTON'S HIGH COOLER

(for one person)
Ice
1 oz. Creme de Cassis
½ cup double-strength Black Currant Tea
Club Soda
Lime or Mint

Fill a tall water glass half full (or half empty for some of you) with ice.

Add Creme de Cassis and tea. Fill the remainder of glass with club soda.

Garnish with a slice of lime or a sprig of mint.

This one is so brisk and refreshing it could even make Rhett turn Scarlett.

ARTICHOKE BALLS

1 lg. can Artichoke Hearts, drained and finely chopped
4 toes Garlic, minced
6 bsp. Olive Oil
1 cup seasoned Bread Crumbs
1 lsp. Parmesan Cheese + ½ cup for "crust"
1 lsp. Romano Cheese + ½ cup for "crust"
2 raw Eggs

Drain artichokes well and chop finely. Sauté artichokes and garlic in olive oil for about three minutes. Add bread crumbs, lsp. cheeses, and cook for another minute. Remove from heat. Whisk raw eggs. Stirring quickly and constantly, turn eggs into artichoke mixture.

Mix together ½ cup each of parmesan and romano cheeses; form artichoke mixture into small balls, then roll the balls in this cheese mixture. Chill until firm.

Submitted by Miss Claire A. Vuoyant

She's kind of new to the drag arena, but Claire catches on faster than a social disease! These artichoke balls will not only have you seeing the future, but might induce you to revisiting some places from your wild past.

MIDDLE CLASS MACARONI SALAD

1½ cups Elbow Macaroni, cooked
  and drained
½ cup firm Tomato chunks (optional)
¼ cup Scallions, sliced (optional)
¼ cup processed American Cheese, cubed
½ cup Mayonnaise
1 tsp. prepared Mustard
¼ tsp. Salt
⅛ tsp. Pepper

Put everything into a bowl. Toss. Chill.

Can also be served with as many other pre-packaged, easy-to-fix foods as possible.

Submitted by Miss Delores Delmonico

Kinda makes you want to drive a station wagon and have some kids with biblical first names.

MEAN, GREEN QUEEN EMERALD SOUP

1 Onion, finely chopped
2 bsp. Butter
3 bsp. Flour
2 cups Milk
2 cups well-drained Spinach, cooked
1 cup Consomme
2 cups Light Cream
½ cup Sherry
Salt and Pepper, to taste
1 wtf. Nutmeg
2 bsp. Almonds, chopped and toasted
2 bsp. Parmesan Cheese, grated

In a skillet, sauté onion in butter until tender. Remove, then stir in flour and gradually add milk.

Purée the spinach with consomme and add light cream, sherry, salt, pepper, and nutmeg. Sprinkle almonds or parmesan cheese over the soup.

Submitted by Miss Inna Trailer

Inna T. commands attention with her cooking skills just as she does with her ambulating. Try this one for sure — and practice your favorite dance steps while it's simmering.

MEAT-A-MAN CASSEROLE

2 lbs. chunk Stew Meat
1 med. head Cabbage, chopped coarsely
2 med. Turnips, sliced
2 bsp. Molasses
2 bsp. Caraway Seeds
¼ tsp. Marjoram
2 tsp. Salt
2 cups hot Water

Preheat oven to 350°. Place all ingredients in casserole dish, mix well, and bake for 1½ hours.

Is delicious with mashed potatoes or rice.

Submitted by Miss Polly Morfuss

Polly tells me that she likes throwing a tiny splash of wine over the whole casserole before tossing it all in the oven, but something tells me she likes throwing wine over most anything before tossing it down the hatch!

PURÉE OF POTATO WITH CARROTS

4 lg. Maine Potatoes, pared and cut into
  thin slices
4 med. Carrots, cut into small cubes
Salt, to taste
¼ cup Cream, scalded
2 bsp. Butter at room temperature

Place the potatoes and carrots in a saucepan, and cover with cold water. Add salt, cover, and bring to a boil. Simmer until soft (approximately 10-15 minutes), then drain.

Put saucepan over a high flame, and toss the vegetables a moment to dry.

Remove from heat and mash. Fluff with a fork. Stirring constantly, add the cream. Bring to a quick boil, then remove from flame. Add the butter, bit by bit. Serve immediately.

Submitted by Miss Bertha Vanera

Bertha, who took this name because there are just too many Drag Queens out there already named Bertha Vanation, is a dear old friend, retired from the fast lane. She spends most days baking for under-privileged Drag Queens and often organizes clothing swaps for her friends.

WAY-TO-A-MAN'S-HEART STUFFED ONIONS

8 Spanish Onions
dab of Butter
4 oz. Mushrooms, sliced
½ lb. ground Veal
¼ cup Bread Crumbs
healthy sprinkle of Parsley
1 wtf. Salt
2 generous wtf. Pepper
1 Egg
Beef Stock

Parboil onions for ½ hour, then drain and dunk in cold water. Scoop out the insides enough so that each can receive a healthy spoonful of stuffing.

Chop the scoopings and fry in butter until light brown, along with mushrooms. Mix in veal, bread crumbs, and parsley. Season with salt and pepper. Mix in egg.

Spoon mixture into each onion and place in oven dish containing beef stock to cover a quarter of the way up on the onions. Top with bread crumbs, cover, and bake at 325° for about one hour.

Submitted by Miss Sissy Blush

Of course, Sissy dearest, even if you reach your man's heart through this recipe, he'll have onion breath for days! Pooh! Anyway, try spooning a bit of orange marmalade on each serving for a great glaze.

TEA SOUFFLÉ

1 oz. Butter
1 oz. Flour
3 bsp. Milk
1 teacupful of strong, prepared Tea
2 oz. Sugar
4 Egg Yolks, stiffly beaten
5 Egg Whites
pinch of Salt
1 oz. Butter
2 bsp. Confectioner's Sugar

Mix butter and flour into a roux. Add milk to moisten further, then gradually add tea, stirring to get a thick sauce.

Stir in sugar and heat on medium-low for five minutes. Let cool slightly, then add egg yolks.

Whip egg whites with pinch (ouch!) of salt until firm but not too stiff (this is a delicate stage of preparation so no obvious jokes will be inserted here).

Prepare your soufflé dish by greasing with butter and dusting it with confectioner's sugar.

Fold the egg whites into the sauce carefully and don't worry if it looks marbled.

Pour mixture into soufflé dish and bake at 400° until it rises well (you may now insert a joke) – about 35-40 minutes.

Glaze or drip icing over the soufflé before serving.

Submitted by Miss Fanci Schmantze

After reading all those "firm," "stiff" and "rising" references, even the most serious of cooks can get quite frustrated and perhaps, anxious. Take it all out while beating those egg yolks!

DIVA DINNA'

Ding Dong! It's those delicious dames from the inner ring of your social vortex, all waddling on in for a special soirée of high-quality, high-class, high-hair happenings.

A bit of light conversation, a heavy serving of compliments to each guest, and a spread that will weigh them down for the evening altogether compromises the formula for a night of girth-meets-mirth group gaiety. As the enjoyment and chatter accelerate, you'll see that "pass the dish" refers to more than table service!

The soft, sensitive tones of Maria Callas (who ain't no chick from Dallas) in the background generates some nice ambiance music. And pop in a grand, diva-worthy flick such as "Madame X" or "Sunset Boulevard" for entertainment. Just make certain you have comfy seating for this Caftans-R-Us crowd.

If you and your gal-pals are in that too-old-for-disco candy though not-quite-ready-for-institution pablum phase of your lives, this meal concept is designed especially for you. Just make sure those servings are all bite-size...whoops! Looks like Miss Maxine Padd has got herself a choker. Give her the Heimlich, Nappi!

FAMILY RECIPE FOR DANDELION WINE

1 qt. Dandelion Blossoms, firmly packed in
a jar
4 qts. Water
1 Yeast Cake
½ additional cup Water
1 lb. seeded Raisins
6 cups Sugar
1 Lemon and 1 Orange, cut into small pieces
with rinds left on
½ pint Rum (perhaps more depending on the
crowd you run with)

(Note: This takes two weeks to prepare, so plan ahead.)

Place blossoms with water in a large kettle and boil slowly for about 30 minutes. Run through a strainer, and then a cheesecloth, into a large stone jar. Once cooled, add yeast cake dissolved in the ½ cup water. Add raisins, sugar, lemon, and orange.

Stir daily for two weeks. Strain and let stand one day for settling. Strain again until clear. Add rum, bottle, and seal.

Serve in a Brandy snifter – the bigger the better.

Submitted by Miss Judy Jetsteins

Although Judy is a metropolitan-type, one of the best times we ever had together was at her upstate New York house where we held a Dandelion Festival. It included everyone picking the blossoms, making the wine (which partygoers later took home to finish), and the crowning of a Dandelion Princess (based on who could come up with the best dandelion whine) who got to wear a dandelion chain all evening.

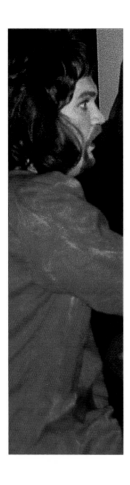

COCOA VAN (A CHICKEN DISH)

1/4 cup Flour
1 lsp. Poultry Seasoning
1 lg. frying Chicken, cut into 8 pieces
1/8 lb. Butter
2 oz. Brandy
1 clove Garlic
1 Bay Leaf
1 thick slice of Ham, cut into 1/2" cubes
1 pinch Thyme
1 bsp. Parsley, chopped
12 sm. white Onions
1/2 lb. Mushrooms, sliced into "T's"
1 cup Chablis, warmed
Salt and Pepper, to taste

Put the flour with poultry seasoning into a brown paper bag, followed by the chicken pieces, two at a time. Shake (the bag) to coat pieces evenly. Melt the butter in a large skillet; sear the chicken pieces on all sides until they are brown. Pour brandy over the chicken and carefully (sleeves back, girls) light a fire with a match. Flame the chicken and brandy for a few seconds and as flames die down, place the lid on the skillet.

Add all other ingredients. Cover and simmer until the chicken is tender. Discard bay leaf.

Mix about 1 bsp. additional butter with one bsp. flour. Gradually mix with the gravy, stirring to avoid lumps. Taste and correct seasoning.

Can be served very hot with rice or egg noodles and a green vegetable.

Submitted by Miss Francesca Frittata

From Francesca: "The way you tacky bitches drink, you'd better make this hours ahead of time. It tastes better reheated, anyhow. Cheers!" (Incidentally, she never did explain to me how this dish got its name — it has nothing to do with vans and it has absolutely no chocolate flavor whatsoever...)

HOT CRABMEAT DIP

1 8 oz. package Cream Cheese
1 sm. can Crabmeat
juice of 1/2 of a fresh Lemon, squeezed by hand
1 wtf. Worcestershire Sauce
1 wtf. Garlic Powder
1 wtf. Salt and Pepper
1 wtf. Monosodium Glutamate

Let cream cheese soften, then add all other remaining ingredients. Preheat oven to 350°, then bake mixture 20 minutes, or until bubbly.

Submitted by Miss Lisa Carr

Lisa sez: For variety, before baking Crabmeat Dip, spread on party rye rounds, sprinkle paprika on top, and place under the broiler until slightly brown.

LEEK MOUSSE

3 lbs. Leeks
3 bsp. Butter
coarse Salt
fresh Pepper
¼ cup Crème Fraîche
1 wtf. Nutmeg
edible Greenery

"Ya trim ends of stalks from the leeks, removing all flaccid parts. Rinse erect leek parts thoroughly and ya chop into ½" pieces. Ya rinse some mo'.

Ya heat the butter in a casserole dish, then add the leeks a few at a time; ya sauté until soft. Season with salt and pepper.

Purée leek mixture in a food processor with crème fraîche, until smooth. Add nutmeg.

Ya pour into serving dishes and decorate with cut-up pieces of a leaf, or any other edible greenery.

Real elegant."

Submitted by Miss Shirley U. Jeste

Seems that the salt isn't the only coarse thing about Shirley and her concoction. Shirley is a newcomer to the illusions circuit, but claims to be no novice in the kitchen. After dictating the recipe to me (I hope I conveyed it as accurately as possible) she noted that this dish goes great alongside most any main course.

RATATOUILLE A LA DE MARCO

¾ cup Onions, thinly-sliced
2 cloves Garlic, crushed
⅓ cup Olive Oil
4 Green Peppers, julienned
2½ cups Eggplant, diced
3 cups Zucchini, sliced
2 cups Tomatoes, peeled and chopped
Salt and Pepper

Sauté onions and garlic in olive oil. Remove and arrange them in layers in a pot along with layers of pepper, eggplant, zucchini, and tomatoes, adding salt and pepper to each layer. Sprinkle with olive oil and simmer, covered, between 35-45 minutes.

Uncover and heat ten minutes.

May be served hot or cold. Is good tossed with pasta and baked with parmesan cheese topping.

Submitted by Miss Connie De Marco

Miss De Marco actually is eye-tailan, but somewhere picked up this recipe for a French dish. (Perhaps it was from a French sailor she also picked up as he wandered the waterfront seeking the warm affections and infinite cleavage that only Miss De Marco could provide.)

CREPES A LA PORNA

So simple!
¾ cup Flour
1 lg. Egg
1 wtf. Salt, to taste
1⅓ cups Milk
2 bsp. Butter, melted

In a mixing bowl dump flour, egg, and salt. Stir in milk with a wire whisk.* Stir in the melted butter.

Over medium heat, warm a crepe-type pan and add a thin layer of crepe ooze mixture to cover the bottom (each crepe should be about 5" diameter). Cook quickly and turn – cook quickly on flip side and remove.

Serve the crepes filled with ice cream, with fruit, or chocolate sauce over it. Yummy!

You may also fill crepes with your favorite fruit or vegetable dishes (for example: strawberry, asparagus, banana, broccoli and garlic, creamed spinach, etc.) and top with sauce (hollandaise, cream sauce, rum sauce, brandy sauce, sugar, cheese sauce, etc.). Be creative, but I find the spicier the filling, the better the overall taste.

*a clean wig brush will also work

Submitted by Miss Porna May

One of the caringest, most sincere hostesses I've ever known, Porna May aims to please. One time she even donned a mini-skirted maid's uniform at her own party to better serve her guests.

SLUMBER PARTY

Fun things to do:

1. Scavenger Hunt: fuzzy slippers, polyester bathrobes, p.j.'s, teddy bears (or even just plain teddies), dippety-do, rollers, emery boards, etc.;

2. Teen Talk: topics such as boy talk, clothing, dumb parent stories, scary date stories;

3. Games: Mystery Boyfriend, Bathrobe Twister, Truth or Wear;

4. Telephone Crank Calls;

5. Home perms, fun fingernails, pretty pedicures, bikini waxes, facials, make-overs.

You probably didn't have this much fun when you really were a teen! The food and snacks — what a menu combo! — are intended for the bunch of adolescent dieters you and your chums are this evening. Go ahead, eat it all, then enjoy one final party event before lights-out: crowd around that porcelain canister, fingers poised — one, two, three...it's a girl-hurl!

SWEET DREAMS

½ part Gin
¼ part Cream
¼ part Lemon Juice
splash of Grenadine

Shake gin, cream, and lemon juice with grenadine.
Serve in a highball glass.

Great for sipping late at night in your porch swing.

MIGHTY NICE CLAM DIP

½ clove Garlic
8 oz. package Cream Cheese
2 tsp. Lemon juice
1½ tsp. Worcestershire Sauce
½ tsp. Salt
fresh Ground Pepper
½ cup Clams, drained and minced
¼ cup Clam Broth

Rub the dip bowl with garlic. In the same bowl
blend all remaining ingredients. Beat until
smooth.

Simple, no?

Great with vegetables or crackers.

Submitted by Miss Tierra Del Fonga

*Miss T. says she puts this on the table and an old Bette
Davis movie in the VCR. Then, while the guests go
ga-ga devouring everything, you'll have time to take a hot
bath before starting dinner.*

QUICHE LORRAINE

3 Eggs
1¾ cups light Cream (half & half)
¾ lb. Swiss Cheese, grated
2 bsp. Onions, minced
1 lsp. Worcestershire Sauce
1 lsp. Salt
1 wtf. Cayenne pepper
¾ cup Ham or Bacon, chopped
1 9" Pie Pastry, ready-made
Parmesan Cheese, grated

Preheat oven to 450°. Beat eggs and add light cream, swiss cheese, onions, worcestershire sauce, salt, and cayenne. Add ham or bacon. Mix well and pour into pastry. Sprinkle with parmesan cheese. Bake for 15 minutes. Reduce heat to 300°. Bake until set, about 45 minutes.

Submitted by Miss Bundla Joy

PORCUPINE MEATBALLS

½ cup Rice, uncooked
1 lb. Ground Beef
1½ lsp. Salt
¼ lsp. Pepper
2 bsp. Onion, minced
3 bsp. Fat
1 cup condensed Tomato Soup
1 cup hot Water
1 Bay Leaf
1 wtf. ground Cloves

Mix together rice, beef, salt, pepper, and onion. Shape into 12 balls.

Brown balls with fat in frying pan. Add tomato soup, water, and bay leaf.

Sprinkle cloves into liquid, cover, and cook 1½ hours over low heat until rice is tender.

Make extra rice to serve with the meatballs.

Submitted by Miss Patty O' Furniture

Assuming she really is Irish, I wonder if this recipe also finds its origins in the Emerald Isle. For that matter, I wonder how much time dear Patty spends on the emerald aisle at Zolan's Jewelry store.

CREAM OF ASPARAGUS SOUP

1 10 oz. package frozen Asparagus Spears
1 cup Water
¼ cup Onion, chopped
2 bsp. Butter
2 bsp. all-purpose Flour
1 cup Milk
1 cup Half & Half
Salt, to taste
½ lsp. white Pepper

Combine first 3 ingredients in a saucepan and bring them to a boil. Cover and reduce heat, simmering until tender, about five minutes. Drain well. Purée asparagus until smooth.

Melt butter over low heat. Add flour, stirring until smooth. Cook one minute. Gradually add milk and half & half on medium heat until bubbly. Stir in asparagus purée, salt and pepper.

Submitted by Miss Rita M. Weep

POTATO FLAPJACKS

3 med. Potatoes
3 Eggs, beaten
½ lsp. Salt
¼ lsp. fresh Pepper
1 lsp. fresh Ginger
Safflower Oil

Peel and grate potatoes. Place in a bowl and cover with cold water, stirring with hands to rinse. Remove and dry on a towel. Let bowl stand about five minutes until the starch settles to bottom, then pour off water, but leave the starch in the bowl.

Return the potatoes to bowl. Add eggs, salt, pepper, and ginger. Stir.

In a large skillet, warm ¼" safflower oil on moderately high heat. Drip in heaping little spoonfuls and flatten with a spoon to make 4" diameter pancakes. Fry until browned (about six minutes).

Keep warm in oven until serving time.

Submitted by Miss Flat-Back Betty

Betty says these are delicious with beef dishes and she loves to add a little spoonful of currant jam or a portion of red cabbage alongside. Thanks for staying vertical long enough to copy this recipe for us, Betty!

JELL-O LOVE

1 package Jell-O (preferably lemon or lime)
1 cup hot Water
¾ cup Juice from fruit below
1 3 oz. package Cream Cheese
1 cup Fruit, drained (such as Fruit Cocktail,
  Pears, or Mandarin Oranges)
1 cup Whipped Cream

Dissolve Jell-O in hot water and add fruit juice. Slowly add cream cheese, blending until smooth. Chill until slightly thickened. Then add fruit and fold in whipped cream.

Pour into a mold and chill until firm.

Unmold and serve on lettuce with fruit garnishes.

Submitted by Miss Anita Mann

Well, one might say it takes real blue-ribbon trailer trash to come up with a good Jell-O recipe. But I always say a good Jell-O recipe is just like a good Drag Queen: artificial in most ways, abundant in components, and fruity as an orchard!

77

Photo by Kerri McCaffery

MAY DAY PICNIC

Won't you have a ball riding around town with a bullhorn, inviting guests to this impromptu day at the park! Simply shriek, "May Day! May Day!," in front of each of your girlfriend's homes and that'll be their signal to join the action. The fun of having a bullhorn is that lots of other people (some perhaps in uniform!) might suddenly be arriving as well.

You'll want to have plenty of party games, so be sure you know all the usual May Day events. First, there's the May Pole dance, a fun fertility rite where you dance, sign, and kick really high around the pole.

Of course, May Day also celebrates the International Day of the Worker, so here are some fun, outdoor communist activities you can enjoy:

1. Pass out hammers and sickles to all attendees and see who can make accessories of them first.

2. Make a game out of filling in the following blank, seeing who can come up with the wittiest line: "From each according to her abilities, to each according to her _____."*
(e.g. dress size, need for attention, etc.)

If you wake up to boom-boom thundershowers on May 1st, don't despair. Save everything for just a few days and reconvene on the 5th for a dandy Cinco de Mayo Chicken Fry-O.

*Karla Marx and Fluffy Engels

SIMPLE POTATO SALAD WITH YOGURT

1 bsp. Vinegar
½ cup raw Carrots, shredded
½ cup Cucumbers, chopped
1 cup plain Yogurt
Salt and Pepper
6 Potatoes, boiled and sliced
Parsley to garnish

Combine everything except potatoes and parsely. Carefully toss potatoes with mixture.

Serve garnished with parsley.

Submitted by Miss Eileen Dover

I first met Eileen by telephone when she responded to my advertisement calling for recipes. Eileen, who claims to have a twin brother Ben, was simply a cornucopia of information and we hit it off so well that I am already planning to visit her and tour the Betsy Ross Historical Home in Philadelphia whenever I next am there.

SANGRIA TIA

1 bottle dry, red Wine
2 Oranges, juice and rind only
1 Lemon, juice and rind only
¼ cup super fine Sugar
2 jiggers Brandy, Curacao, or Cointreau
1 wtf. ground Clove
1 wtf. Allspice
Ice Cubes

Combine in a tacky, plastic barroom pitcher: wine, juice and rinds of oranges and lemon, sugar, brandy (or curacao or Cointreau), clove, and allspice. Fill remainder of pitcher with ice cubes and stir. Serve in wine glasses.

This will knock the knickers off of those tawdry wine coolers any day.

FUN WITH MELONS

1 lg. Cantaloupe
2 bsp. Butter
½ lb. lean Ground Beef or Lamb
1 med. Onion, finely chopped
½ cup long-grain White Rice, uncooked
¼ cup Pine Nuts
¼ cup dried Currants
1½ bsp. Sugar (optional)
¼ tsp. Cinnamon
Salt, to taste
1 cup Water

Cut off 1" at the top of the melon and set piece aside. Using a long-handled spoon, clean the inside of the melon, creating a gourd (I've always loved that word – gourd), throwing away the seeds. Using a long-handled spoon, scoop out one cup of the center pulp and chop.

In a heavy skillet, warm the butter over moderate heat. Add the meat and onions; sauté until brown, stirring frequently. Add the rice, pine nuts, currants, one bsp. sugar, cinnamon, salt, chopped melon pulp, and water. Mix well.

Cool until the liquid in the pan is absorbed, stirring occasionally. Remove from the heat and let cool to room temperature.

Sprinkle the inner parts of the melon with the remaining ½ bsp. of sugar and spoon the meat stuffing into it. Cover with the reserved piece of melon and secure with wooden picks. Place in an oiled baking pan just large enough to hold the melon comfortably.

Bake in a preheated 350° oven one hour or until tender.

Submitted by Miss Mocha De Lait

Fun, indeed! When I received this recipe submission from Mocha, who lives in the Cleveland area, I tried to call her for the correct pronunciation of the last name – is it "De-light" or "De-Lay" I wonder? Her line was busy both times and my patience ran out (Mocha doesn't know about Honey's "Two Fluffs and You're Out" rule), so we may never know just what to call her. On the other hand, I call her recipe exciting and unusual, something for you to try the next time you really want to impress.

WIENER WONDERS

6 Weenies
6 slices Bread, toasted
American or Cheddar Cheese, sliced
Tomato slices
Onion slices

Slice weenies lengthwise and place under oven broiler until brown.

Place on top of toast slice and add cheese, tomato, and onion slice (in that order) on each. Put under broiler briefly until cheese is melted.

May be served with beer and hash browns as well.

Submitted by Miss Sharon Needle

BEEFY CHILI

2 lbs. Ground Beef (DO NOT SUBSTITUTE!)
1 toe Garlic, minced
1 Onion, diced
2 cans of ranch style Beans
1 sm. can of Green Chilies
Spices (add various items at will...like chili
    powder, salt, etc.)

First, brown the meat – BEEF – (this has nothing to do with nude sunbathing). If your meat – BEEF – is a bit "old" its a good idea to add granulated garlic or garlic salt during the browning step to kill that old feet smell. Add diced onion to the browning meat – BEEF – and cook 'til well done. You may opt to drain off excess grease at this time...or not. Open the cans of beans and chili and add to the meat – BEEF – and continue cooking until thoroughly heated throughout.

Additional toppings would include sour cream, cheese, fried eggs, or additional BEEF products.

Submitted by Miss Thelma Jo

Thelma Jo isn't actually a Drag Queen, but the mother of a close friend, Sofonda Cox (of whom I am sure she's very proud) of New Orleans, and is originally from New Mexico, where Thelma Jo was President of the Beefy Border Belles.

ONE-EYED BURGERS

1 lb. Ground Beef
½ Onion, chopped
3 generous squirts Ketchup
1 tsp. Beef Flavoring (powdered gravy or bullion)
Salt and Pepper
4 6" slices French Bread, toasted
4 Eggs
1 sm. jar Capers

Mix all of the above, except bread, eggs, and capers, and divide into four burger patties. Cook slowly, draining fat after five minutes, but leaving any fat that remains after that.

Remove patties once cooked and place on slice of toasted french bread.

In the remaining fat, fry the eggs. Note that they are best with the whites cooked and the yolks somewhat runny. If you want to act French and have the stomach for it, you may also use raw egg yolks.

Place eggs on each burger and sprinkle yolk with 4-5 capers.

Garnish nicely. Good with pickled beets and your best french fries.

Submitted by Miss Angie-of-the-North

Detroit's Angie-of-the-North has a wonderful lounge act which you can catch in certain suburban venues. And speaking of capers, if ever you meet Angie, ask her about the caper she once tried to pull in the lingerie section of Hudson's Department Store.

EARLY AMERICAN CORN PUDDIN'

2½ cups cream-style Corn
5 bsp. Flour
1 bsp. Sugar
1 tsp. Salt
¼ cup Butter, melted
¾ cup Milk
3 Eggs, beaten

Using a wire whisk, mix corn and flour. Add the other ingredients, mixing well.

Bake in a greased, two-quart casserole dish at 325° for one hour.

Submitted by Miss Diamondtina

I wonder if Miss D's family brought this classic recipe over on the Mayflower when they came three generations ago.

PINEAPPLE BANANA FRITTERS

1⅓ cups all-purpose Flour
1½ tsp. double-acting Baking Powder
3 bsp. granulated Sugar
1 tsp. Ginger, ground
pinch of Salt
¾ cup fresh Pineapple, chopped and drained
¾ cup Banana, chopped
½ cup cold Milk
1 lg. Egg, beaten lightly
1 cup Vegetable Oil
½ cup Confectioner's Sugar

Sift flour, baking powder, sugar, ginger, and salt together into a small bowl. In another bowl combine the pineapple, banana, milk, and egg; add the flour mixture and stir until everything is combined.

In a skillet heat 1½" of oil and drop batter in by spoonfuls, turning the fritters.

When golden, the fritters should be removed with a slotted spoon and placed on a paper towel to dry.

Sift confectioner's sugar over them lightly.

Serve warm.

Can also be great alongside chicken dishes and steamed green beans.

Submitted by Miss Flicka De Tong

Wear something equally bright and festive — a floral print and topaz rhinestones. Many thanks to my friend Flicka!

PEARL BEFORE SWINE

This little piggy went to market!

Then she dutifully came right home and cooked up a pretty party array for her particularly porcine pals!

Invite a whole variety of your plumpest and perkiest playmates to ensure some real diversity in the crowd. Tell your guests to wear their finest, or even just their most unusual, pearls as creatively as they can.

We've placed our most *different* recipe contributions in this meal theme. If your guests want to, they can just turn up their snouts and say no-no to anything they won't want. Can they say it in pig Latin? And while we're being international, ask if some of your French friends might be squealing "oui, oui, oui – all the way home," later on.

Entertainment may consists of sing-alongs (yes, they can oink if they really wish to) of such favorites as "A Boy Named Sue E.," or "I Got You, Babe," or "Bringin' Home the Bacon." If it's a nicer-size crowd you might want to make the menu a charity affair by passing around a piggy bank before guests leave. Or, have them all bring needles and thread and make the night into an old-fashioned sowing bee...

Photo by Lauri Flaquer

BLOODY MARY

Vegetable Juice
2 wtf. Tabasco
1 tsp. fresh Garlic, minced
1 tsp. fresh Horseradish, minced
1 wtf. Lime Juice
1 pinch ground Pepper
1 wtf. Worcestershire Sauce
2 oz. Vodka
1 stem Celery, Pickled Okra, or Spicy Green Bean

Mix all ingredients and swish, over ice, with celery, okra, or green bean (you can even use all three!).

Submitted by Miss Dare E. Queen

TEA EGGS

8 Eggs
3 bsp. Black Tea Leaves
1 Cinnamon Stick
3 whole Star Anise
1 bsp. Salt
preserved Ginger

Boil eggs in water for ten minutes; drain and let stand in cold water until cool. Crack shells but do not peel. Place eggs, in one layer, in a saucepan with tea leaves, cinnamon stick, star anise, and salt. Cover with water and cook over low heat for one hour. Remove from heat and let cool in tea water. Shell and serve whole or halved with preserved ginger.

Submitted by Miss Caprice McPoodle

Caprice is a sweet old friend of mine who owns a collection of jewelry not to be believed. Some of those rocks are the size of Tippi Hedron's back splats, I tell you! Oh, to be locked in that safe deposit box for just one night...

PEAS 'N PEANUT SALAD

1 10 oz. package Frozen Peas, cooked slightly
1 cup Cocktail Peanuts
¼ cup Onion, chopped
½ cup Celery, chopped
½ cup Mayonnaise
⅓ cup Sour Cream
½ tsp. Salt
1 healthy wtf. Pepper (watch those limp wrists, ladies!)
1 tsp. Worcestershire sauce
6 slices Bacon, cooked and crumbled

Couldn't be easier – mix everything. Serve.

Submitted by Miss Jessica Helms

It's more than coincidence that Miss Jessica Helms hails from the Tarheel state (not to be confused with the High-heel state) just like another Helms. Rumor has it that she once decided to challenge the old turd by running for public office. Well, in the end, the only running to be done was by Miss Jessica Helms herself, right out of town and across state lines to Tennessee, handbag and all.

CRAB-SHRIMP CHOWDER

1 can Tomato Soup
1 can Cream of Mushroom Soup
1 soup can Half & Half
2 bsp. Celery, chopped
2 bsp. Parsley, chopped
2 bsp. Shallots, chopped
1 lb. Crabmeat
1 lb. Shrimp, cooked
1 bsp. Bourbon
Worcestershire Sauce, to taste
Tabasco, to taste

Put tomato and mushroom soups, milk, celery, parsley, and shallots in saucepan and cook until vegetables are tender. Add crabmeat and shrimp. Cook until good and hot, but do not boil. Just before serving, add the bourbon, worcestershire, and Tabasco. Serve in soup plates over cooked rice.

Submitted by Miss Mary Ellen Staircase

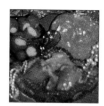

GRILLED LAMB'S HEAD

1 Lamb's Head
Eggs, beaten
Bread Crumbs
Flour
Salt
plenty of Butter
variety of Vegetables
sm. Potatoes, boiled

Have the butcher cut lamb's head in two (one half head is sufficient per dinner guest). Clean carefully and soak the parts in salt water for a few hours.

Place in fresh water to cook, along with the tongue, and simmer until easy to skin. Be careful when peeling the skin off the head and tongue. Cut out the eyes and ears (be extremely careful not to remove the fat behind the eyes as people insist that this provides the best part of the overall taste).

Remove the palate and split the tongue in two. Dip each piece, as well as the half heads, in beaten eggs and then in bread crumbs blended with flour and salt.

Fry in plenty of butter and serve with a variety of vegetables and small boiled potatoes covered with butter.

Submitted by Miss Virginia Ratzasz

I just had to print this overwhelming recipe, even though it honestly left me speechless (to the point that I don't think I'll ever speak to that bitch Ginnie again!). As I read it over the first time I kept getting a picture of Hannibal Lechter in drag. I really hope to hear from any of you gentle readers daring enough to prepare this dish! Something tells me you'll have to visit Morocco to buy the groceries for it...

BROILED, SKEWERED LAMB

2 lbs. boneless Lamb, trimmed and cut into 1½ - 2" cubes
3 sm. Onions, quartered
3 sm. Tomatoes, quartered
2 med. Green Peppers, quartered and seeded
½ cup Olive Oil
¼ cup dry, red Wine
3 bsp. freshly-squeezed Lemon Juice, strained
2 lg. cloves Garlic, finely chopped
2 lsp. dried Oregano Leaves
2 Bay Leaves, broken into small pieces
1½ lsp. Salt
½ lsp. fresh Black Pepper

Place lamb, onion, tomatoes, and green pepper in a deep bowl. Combine the remaining ingredients and pour marinade over the lamb and vegetables, taking care to coat everything well. Cover and let stand at room temperature two hours or in the refrigerator five to six hours, turning from time to time.

Remove the lamb from marinade and place on long skewers, leaving a few inches at each end. String vegetables on separate skewers, since the cooking time varies. Broil in the oven, or over charcoal, 3-4" from heat, until the vegetables and meat brown evenly on all sides (about 15-20 minutes).

Remove from skewers with fork and serve with rice.

Submitted by Miss Ruby Van Der Douche

Miss Ruby explains that when this dish is made with lamb it's called a Shishka Bob. You can also prepare it with beef (Shishka Chuck) or with Italian sausage (Shishka Tony).

LEEKS WITH VINAIGRETTE

3 dozen leeks (2 bunches)
1 bsp. fresh Lemon Juice
1 bsp. Red Vinegar
1 bsp. prepared Mustard
1/4 bsp. Salt
3-4 bsp. Olive Oil

"Ya take the leeks and ya separate leaves and bulbs. Then ya take off that layer of skin, ya cut the roots and ya toss 'em. Wash leaves and bulbs real good.

In a skillet ya boil salted H₂0 and ya cook the bulbs until as tender as a Judy Garland ballad (about two minutes). Ya drain, ya set 'em aside on a towel to dry. Then ya place the leaves in the H₂0 and boil 30 seconds. Ya dry them, too.

Combine lemon juice, red vinegar, mustard, and salt in a jar. Ya shake. Add olive oil. Ya reshake.

Ya serve."

Submitted by Miss Shirley U. Jeste

Actually, it's no coincidence that both Shirley's entries were for leek recipes since she tells me with pride that she grew up on a leek farm in northern Louisiana. Shirl-girl insists she can't even take a leak without thinking back to that childhood farm (to which I say it's a good thing she didn't grow up by the city dump...)!

SAUERKRAUT (YES, SAUERKRAUT) AND CHOCOLATE CAKE

1 1/2 cups Sugar
2/3 cup Shortening
1 lsp. Vanilla
1/3 lsp. Salt
1/2 cup Cocoa
3 Eggs
2 1/2 cups sifted Flour
1 lsp. Baking Soda
1 lsp. Baking Powder
1 cup Water
1/2 cup Sauerkraut, drained and chopped

Cream sugar and shortening with electric beaters on medium speed for ten minutes. Add vanilla, salt, and cocoa (sounds gross, doesn't it?). Continue beating five minutes on low speed. Add eggs and blend five minutes, or until light.

Sift flour, baking soda, and baking powder together. Add alternately with water, using low speed.

Wash the sauerkraut and add to mixture.

Bake in 13 x 9 x 2 greased/floured pan at 375° for 45 minutes.

Cool and frost with favorite icing.

Submitted by Miss Eva Reddy

Miss Eva hails from the bustling burg of Hat-lanta and there are unconfirmed stories that she claims to be Helen Reddy's illegitimate half-sister. If true, it kind of gives "I Am Woman" some new dementia — I mean dimension (can't you just hear it..."I am woman, hear me roar, with proportions too big to ignore...")! In any case, at first glance I thought this recipe submission was right up there with the unforgettable Grilled Lamb's Head, but this is a real must-try! Go on, give it a whirl, girl!

FEAST OF THE ASSUMPTION SHINDIG

Here's a sample invitation:

Come to Miss _____'s

Feast of the Assumption Shindig

to be held _____

at precisely _____ o'clock.

Party games will include:

Reaching Heavenly Heights (bring wig brush and pins)

Pin the Stigmata on the Virgin

She-Rades (have a favorite Bible character in mind)

❖

Dinner will be served

❖

Dress: Something divinely-inspired

❖

Remember: Always Assume Everything!

Photo by Alison Gootee

HOT SPICED WINE

2 qts. dry, red Wine

2 qts. Muscatel

1 pint Sweet Vermouth

2 cups Raisins

1 Orange Peel

1 bsp. whole Cardamon Seeds, crushed

1 bsp. Cloves

2 Cinnamon Sticks

1½ cups Sugar

1½ cups Vodka

2 cups whole Almonds, blanched

In a 6-8 quart stainless steel pot combine wine, muscatel, sweet vermouth, raisins, orange peel, cardamon seeds, cloves, and cinnamon sticks.

Cover and let stand several hours so that all flavors are absorbed.

Just before serving, add sugar and vodka. Stir well and bring to a full boil over high heat. Remove at once from heat and stir in almonds.

Ladle into mugs. Serves 20-25, or approximately ten Drag Queens.

Submitted by Miss Susia Concepcion

Miss Concepcion relays to me that there is nothing cozier than inviting guests over on a bitterly cold evening, sitting by the fire, cashmere to the hearth, and chatting over mugs of this warm, spiced drink.

SPARKLE'S SHRIMP

2 lbs. boiled Shrimp (40/50 count,
  peeled and deveined)

1 bottle Crab Boil seasoning

1 sm. can Tomato Paste

2 lsp. Scallions, chopped

1 lsp. fresh Basil, finely chopped

wtf. Tabasco

1 lsp. Tarragon Vinegar

1 bsp. Creole Mustard

pinch Chili Powder

Salt and Pepper, to taste

3 oz. white Wine

3 oz. Whipping Cream

½ head Iceberg Lettuce, shredded

1 lg. Tomato, sliced

1 Lemon, sliced

½ bunch Parsley

Place crab-boiled shrimp (drained and cooled) in a bowl. Refrigerate, covered, for 45 minutes. Mix tomato paste, scallions, basil, Tabasco, vinegar, mustard, chili powder, salt, pepper, white wine, and cream in a mixing bowl. Stir until blended, then chill. Place shredded lettuce on a salad plate and top with a tomato slice. Spoon 10 to 12 shrimp with sauce over the tomato slice and garnish with two lemon slices and a parsley sprig and serve.

OTHER USES: Delicious with all seafood, chicken, as a dip, or as a sandwich spread – anything that suits your taste buds.

Submitted by Miss Treasura Sparkle

I'll bet Treasura even cleans her bauble-wear in it.

SPINACH SALAD

    1 lb. Spinach
    1 clove Garlic
    ½ cup Vegetable Oil
    ¼ cup Red Wine Vinegar
    ¼ cup Lemon Juice
    ¼ tsp. Salt
    1 wtf. Pepper
    2 bsp. Parmesan Cheese
    ½ cup Croutons
    2 hard-cooked Eggs, sliced
    6 Bacon Slices, cooked and crumbled

Wash spinach. Discard stems. Tear leaves into bite-size pieces. Chill for two hours. Combine garlic and oil in a glass jar; cover and let stand one hour. Discard garlic. Combine vinegar, lemon juice, salt, pepper, and cheese in a small bowl. Gradually beat in garlic oil, pouring in a thin stream. Pour dressing over spinach. Add croutons. Toss well, garnish with egg slices and bacon.

Submitted by Miss Dorothy Fawcett

Photo by Alison Gootee

TURTLE SOUP

    1½ - 2 lbs. Turtle Meat
    some chopped Ham
    Soda Water
    3 sm. Onions, chopped
    3 Garlic Cloves, chopped
    1 stick Butter
    ¼ tsp. Thyme
    Bay Leaf
    6 bsp. Flour
    1 can Tomatoes
    15 Cloves
    Sherry
    1 hard-boiled Egg, chopped, Parsley, and Lemon
        to garnish

Cut turtle meat and ham into small pieces; soak in soda water. Cover only turtle meat with water; boil slowly, 45 minutes to one hour. Take out and save water. Brown onion and garlic in stick of butter. Add thyme, bay leaf, turtle meat and blend. Add flour, tomatoes, turtle water, and cloves. Cook until meat is tender. Add sherry when served with hard-boiled chopped egg on top with parsley and piece of lemon.

Submitted by Miss Happy Nosegay

HISPANIC RICE

    3 bsp. Bacon Fat
    1 cup Water
    1 cup Rice, uncooked
    ¾ cup Onion, chopped
    ½ cup Green Pepper, chopped
    ½ cup Celery, chopped
    1 14 oz. can stewed Tomatoes
    1½ tsp. Salt
    1 tsp. Chili Powder
    1 Banana
    3 bsp. Coconut Flakes or Raisins
    Parsley, chopped

Heat 2 bsp. bacon fat and water in a large frying pan and add the rice. Stirring, brown rice lightly.

Add remaining fat, onion, green pepper, and celery. Cook until celery is soft.

Add all but banana, coconut, and parsley. Cover pan for ten minutes, add a bit more water, cover and cook until soft.

Just before serving, peel banana and cut into small pieces. Mix banana and coconut flakes with rice. Top with parsley.

Serve with a smile and be prepared to dig out you castanets!

Submitted by Miss Sally Manella

Si Señorita! If frying in bacon fat makes you feel all grimy, do what the Spanish gals do while it's cooling: go scrub yourself well, then apply lots of, what else, oil of olé.

HEAVENLY GINGERED PEARS

2 cups Water
2 cups Sugar
1 inch-long Cinnamon Stick
2 strips of Lemon Peel
½ oz. dried Ginger root
1 tsp. whole Cloves
6 firm Bartlett Pears, peeled and sliced

Combine everything (except pears) in a saucepan and bring to a boil. Then add pears.

Let pears poach until transparent and somewhat tender. Remove from heat and let pears cool in the syrup.

Submitted by Miss Venus de Migraine

When the Venus first came to the United States from Cuba she says she tried to fix this recipe, only she read "gloves" where it said "cloves." Imagine her shredding up her best pair of white lace gloves trying to get a little spoonful!

CHICKEN, DOLCE CHICKEN

2 Chicken Fryers, cut-up
4 bsp. Shortening
1 med. Onion, chopped
2 bsp. Brown Sugar
1 tsp. Salt
¼ cup Water
1 can frozen Orange Juice or Pineapple Juice

Brown chicken in shortening, then remove and place in a single layer in a shallow dish. Sauté onion in the same shortening and add remaining ingredients. Sauté until bubbling. Pour over chicken.

Bake at 350° for one hour.

Can be served with parsleyed rice and a green vegetable.

Submitted by Miss Tiara

Tiara is really a Wall Street businessperson with a family who invented the name in order to qualify for this cookbook. All I can say, Tiara, baby, is that it often seems to start with chicken...

"LEROYS" (CHOCOLATE MOUSSE)

4 oz. unsweetened Chocolate
4 Egg Whites
1 cup Heavy Cream
¾ cup Powdered Sugar

Melt chocolate in a double-boiler over low heat. Then cool to 100° on a candy thermometer.

In a medium bowl beat the egg whites until stiff peaks form (about a minute) using an electric mixer. In another bowl beat cream until foamy (about a minute), also using a mixer. Add sugar and continue beating until soft peaks form — but don't beat too long.

Carefully fold the cream mixture into the egg whites. Add the 100° chocolate, folding it in quickly until well-blended. Spoon into a serving bowl and chill at least two hours.

Submitted by Miss Phyllis Stein

Using a heavily overpacked handbag, I think I might smash a nutty candy bar between sheets of waxed paper and sprinkle it atop this dessert just to give it a final "zingue."

Photo by Kerri McCaffery

ASH BLONDE WEDNESDAY BRUNCH

Ash Wednesday is the day we receive ashes to help atone for some of the naughty, nasty no-no's we have done since last year. Why not create a nice brunch around it?

In fact, why should atonement make us all into a bunch of gloomy, guilty Gretas? Get your girlfriends all lined up in two rows and make an old-fashioned human spanking machine! What fun you'll all have paying penance with this party activity. And it's completely safe — just watch those nails and don't burn your palms!

This can be followed up by a wonderful parlour game like "I Confess" played by the same rules as "I Spy."

The only real rule for the Wednesday Brunch get-together is an ash-blonde stack atop each of the girl's noggins. And why not add a nifty altar boy to serve it all! Food selections are on the lighter side of things (nothing is blackened, contrary to what you might expect). Beverages should be appropriate for the post-Fat Tuesday faces you'll be encountering (think pooch fur).

So it's lashes to lashes, dust to dust. And you'd better get dusting for this event or you'll be paying some nasty social penance, indeed...

ARTICHOKES WITH CRABMEAT AND HOLLANDAISE SAUCE

4 Artichokes
3 bsp. liquid Crab Boil
I bsp. Cooking Oil
3 bsp. Parmesan Cheese
2 bsp. Butter
6 Egg Yolks
½ lb. Crabmeat
3 bsp. Lemon Juice
I lsp. Salt
I pinch Cayenne

Place artichokes in large pot with steam tray. Add crab boil and water halfway to artichokes. Sprinkle cooking oil over artichokes, then sprinkle cheese. Boil until water steams down, about 1-1½ hours.

HOLLANDAISE SAUCE: Mix butter, egg yolks, crabmeat, lemon juice, salt, and cayenne in a saucepan on slow fire. Stir constantly until thickened, about 35 minutes. Dip artichoke leaves in sauce and...yummmmmmmmmm!

Submitted by Miss Goddess Goode

This delightful dame claimed to be the identical twin of Miss Goddess Grate, another recipe contributor. Questions over their differing last names and dimension incompatibilities (Grate measures in at about 6'7" and the diminutive Goode is at best 5'4", poor lass, alas) were quick to put falsies to bed.

HOT TOMATO JUICE

I lg. can spicy Tomato Juice
I sm. Onion, grated
I lsp. Worcestershire Sauce
Salt and Tabasco, to taste
½ cup Heavy Cream, chilled
2 bsp. minced Chives

Combine the tomato juice with the onion, worcestershire sauce, and seasonings. Heat just to the boiling point.

Whip the heavy cream until very stiff. Blend in the chives and add any more salt if needed.

Serve the hot tomato juice with a dollop of the spiced, chilled cream on top.

Great for winter brunches.

Submitted by Miss Chalmatia St. Bernard

On Chalmatia's own turf (down in the Parish) they sometimes add a splash of vawd-ker, but never on Ash Wednesday.

MANDARIN SALAD

1 package miniature Marshmallows
1 16 oz. tub Sour Cream
1 can Mandarin Oranges, drained
¼ cup Walnuts
¼ cup Coconut
¼ cup sliced Cherries

Place marshmallows in large mixing bowl. Fold in sour cream. Let set two hours. In separate bowl, mix other ingredients. Combine with marshmallow mix, stir until well-blended. Better served the day after preparation.

Submitted by Miss Sugar de Bowle

E-Z SAUSAGE/CHICKEN GUMBO

1 lb. Smoked Sausage, cut into 1" pieces
1 Onion, chopped
1 tsp. decent Cooking Oil
1 lg. can Stewed Tomatoes
1 can Okra, drained
1 can Chunky Chicken/Vegetable Soup
Salt, Pepper, and crushed Garlic, to taste

Saute sausage with onion in cooking oil until onions slightly tender (this is the hardest part). Pour in cans of tomato, okra, and soup. Simmer. Add salt, pepper, and crushed garlic.

Serve with a big scoop of rice in each bowl.

Submitted by Miss Teri Parkway

Ms. P., named after a strip of autoroute in New Orleans, is quite the gal on the go — and I think it shows through in her recipe. I haven't had the chance (or stomach) to attempt this culinary quickie, but off the top of my head recommend it most to those of you who are more of the trailer tradition.

GARLIC ROAST POTATOES

3 lbs. sm. red Potatoes, quartered and
    unpeeled
¾ cup Olive Oil
4 bsp. Butter
12 cloves Garlic, minced
Salt and Pepper
Italian flat-leaf Parsley

Preheat over to 400°. Toss ingredients together and spread on a roasting pan. Roast 30-40 minutes, tossing potatoes once or twice until they are brown and just tender. Accesorize with parsley. Serves 8-12.

Submitted by Miss Vulva Moe Beaumont

HUEVOS DIVINOS

1 bsp. Cooking Oil

1 Green Pepper, chopped

½ Onion, chopped

3 cloves Garlic, peeled and chopped

1 wtf. white Wine

5 Eggs

1 15 oz. can Tomato Sauce

Salt and Pepper

Oregano

5 English Muffins

In a frying pan heat, on medium high, the cooking oil. Stir in green pepper, onion, and garlic. Add a wtf. of white wine and stir over medium heat until vegetables are semi-tender.

Carefully break eggs atop vegetables and cook covered on medium heat one minute. Add tomato sauce, being sure to distribute it evenly throughout the skillet. Sprinkle salt, pepper, and oregano over the sauce.

Reduce heat to low and continue cooking, covered, until eggs are at desired doneness.

Serve whole eggs on english muffins (you could substitute toast or thinly-sliced grain bread).

Submitted by Miss Delilah Gillette

Delilah used to own and operate the Clip 'N Chat Beauty Salon in Miami. I first tasted this dish at a brunch she gave and haven't forgotten it since. Bless your shears, Deli!

CHOCOLATE BARF COOKIES

½ cup Sugar

½ cup Shortening

½ cup Cottage Cheese

1 Egg

¼ lsp. Vanilla

¼ cup Cocoa

1¼ cups Flour

½ lsp. Baking Powder

½ lsp. Baking Soda

¼ lsp. Salt

Cream sugar and shortening. Add cottage cheese, egg, vanilla, and cocoa. Beat well. Add flour, baking powder, baking soda, and salt. Mix well. Drop with a lsp. on a greased cookie sheet. Bake at 350° for 10-12 minutes.

Submitted by Miss Virginia Hamm

Ol' Virginia really is the queen of matching unusual ingredients. I guess if you could see some of the types she's paired herself with, the recipes wouldn't seem so unusual...on the other hand, cottage cheese and cocoa together are right up there with Grilled Lamb's Head and Sauerkraut Cake.

OUTDOOR BARBIE-Q

First, find yourself a little toy Ken doll to work the grill. Flipping, squashing, and spatula matters in general must stay in his domain.

Next, assemble your most Barbie-esque pals for a real afternoon of girl games in the park. The girls needn't fuss and fret too, too much about looking like real Barbie dolls, since the ones you buy in the store aren't anatomically correct, either.

To keep the activities going, divide the gang into two groups. Those who want to stay out of harmful ray's way can play Old Maid under a tent awning. The ruddier and rowdier bunch get to jump rope! Help them out be providing standard children's rhymes they can recite as they skip, such as:

> Drig, drag
> Sent to school in rags
> 'Cause Mama bought a brand new Buick.
> Got me some Elmer's and got me some shears,
> Now teacher's missing drapes, but I have gowns for years!

Shrimp's on the barbie! Uh-oh, looks more like the Barbies are on the shrimp!

Photo by Alison Gootee

CHILLED YOGURT-CUCUMBER SOUP

2 med. Cucumbers (about ½ lb. each)

4 cups Plain Yogurt

¾ cups Ice Water

Salt, to taste

2 bsp. fresh Mint Leaves, finely chopped

2 bsp. Scallions (including about 2" of the green tops), finely chopped

¾ cups Ice, crushed

Peel cukes and cut lengthwise into eighths. Cut out and discard any large seeds. Slice cukes crosswise into ¼" pieces.

Pour yogurt into a deep bowl and stir with a large spoon until smooth. Add ice water and blend carefully, yet completely. Add cukes and salt; stir well.

Sprinkle mint, scallions, and crushed ice on soup just before serving. Serve in individual bowls.

Submitted by Miss Vicki Di Vine

Sounds like a great idea for a Sunday in summer, Vicki, dear. Also sounds a bit exotic for a gal who's never left New Jersey and who thinks the Middle East lies somewhere around Weehawken.

SHANDY

½ part Dark Beer

½ part dry, very cold Ginger Ale

Mix in a large glass. No garnish needed.

I love a Shandy because I can mix it myself at the bar (sometimes I'll even bring a small flask of ginger ale in my clutch!). This drink is popular in Europe, but you pretentious pretties already knew that.

95

BARBECUE SHRIMP

7 to 8 lbs. lg. Shrimp
2 sticks Butter
1 cup Olive Oil
½ cup Chili Sauce
¼ cup Worcestershire Sauce
2 Lemons, thinly sliced
4 cloves Garlic, minced
4 bsp. Lemon Juice
1 bsp. minced Parsley
2 lsp. Paprika
2 lsp. Oregano
3 lsp. red Cayenne Pepper
1 lsp. Tabasco
2 bsp. Liquid Smoke
Salt and Pepper, to taste

Wash the shrimp well and spread out in a shallow pan. Combine all of the ingredients above in a sauce pan over low heat. Let simmer for ten minutes, then pour over the shrimp. Mix well and refrigerate for two to three hours. Baste and turn the shrimp every 30 minutes.

Preheat the oven to 300° and bake the shrimp for 30 minutes, turning them at least every ten minutes.

This can be served in a soup bowl with chunks of French bread to sop up the sauce.

Submitted by Miss Martha Motor

Martha is just an itty-bitty thing from Atlanta by way of New Orleans, St. Louis, and numerous truck stops in-between.

SPECIAL SALSA

4-6 lg. Tomatoes
1 bunch Cilantro
1 Lime, juice only
1 Lemon, juice only
crushed Peppers (dried in a shaker)
Garlic Salt
Salt and Pepper
2 bunches Scallions

Cut tomatoes in sections of four. Cut stems off cilantro. Squeeze lemon and lime juice in.

Mix in a blender. Add peppers, garlic salt, salt, and pepper to desired taste. Mix again.

Pour into a large bowl and add cut scallions. Mix with a spoon.

Delicious with tortilla chips, on chicken, eggs... anything!

Submitted by Miss Guyo

Miss Guyo is actually an internationally-acclaimed persona and I think that any recipe she takes time out to contribute is definitely worth a try!

FAVORITE CHICKEN SALAD

3 Chicken Breasts (6 halves), cut in bite sized
pieces
1 lg. can Pineapple Chunks, drained (save juice)
1½ cups chopped Celery (not diced, but
chunkier)
1 cup Cashew or Walnuts
3 lg. Red Delicious Apples, leave skin on, chopped
in chunks and dipped in pineapple juice so
they won't discolor
Mayonnaise, mixed with lemon juice

Cook chicken by baking in dutch oven in water at 350° for 45-60 minutes. Mix all chunck ingredients in large bowl (including chicken). Just before serving, toss with mayonnaise. Serve.

Especially good when served with croissants and melon.

Submitted by Miss Mammary Lane

MARINATED BEEF STEAK

¼ cup Onion, minced

2 bsp. Parsley, chopped

2 lsp. White Vinegar

1 bsp. Dijon Mustard

1 clove Garlic, minced

½ lsp. dried Thyme Leaves

1 wtf. Soy Sauce

1 lb. Beef Chuck Shoulder Steak

Stir together all ingredients that never mooed. Place whatever once mooed in a plastic bag and add nonmooing ingredients, spreading evenly on all sides. Seal bag and leave in fridge at least six hours, turning once or more.

Get rid of marinade and place steak on rack in a broiler pan with meat 3-4" from heat. Broil about 16 minutes (longer if you like it well-done) turning once.

Carve into slices. Serves one to four, depending on appetite.

Submitted by Miss Anita Mann

And we thought steaks were only for lumberjack types!

MASHED TURNIP CASSEROLE

2½ lbs. Turnips, boiled, peeled, and cubed

1 med. package Cream Cheese

½ cup Milk

2 bsp. Butter or Margarine

¼ lsp. Garlic Powder

¼ lsp. Salt

ground Nutmeg

Mash turnips while hot and blend with all other ingredients, except nutmeg.

Pour into casserole dish and sprinkle with ground nutmeg. Bake at 350° for 30-45 minutes.

Submitted by Miss Polly Morfuss

Oooh! Turnip the heat and plunk this baby into your oven! I think parsley garnishes would make it all pretty-like, too!

SKIPPER'S NIGHT OFF CORNMEAL COOKIES

1 Egg, beaten

1 6 oz. container Peach Yogurt

½ cup packed Brown Sugar

½ cup Margarine

1 cup Unbleached Flour

1 cup Cornmeal

½ lsp. Baking Soda

½ lsp. ground Nutmeg

¼ lsp. Baking Powder

Preheat oven to 375°. Mix egg, yogurt, brown sugar, and margarine in a medium-sized bowl. Stir in the remaining ingredients.

Drop dough by rounded littlespoons onto ungreased cookie sheets. Bake 6-8 minutes, or until light brown.

Submitted by Miss Toya Makes

Oh boya, Miss Toya! You've got a way with those sweets. Now to get that old hearse you drive fixed!

COME AS YOU AREN'T PARTY ———————————

    Allright, allright, if you're a drag-doer it means you're already parading around no-telling where as something you already aren't. This meal/party theme maximizes that and invites you to incorporate objects d'art, d'Henri, d'Edouard, and d'anybody else who's got nifty stuff.

    A jalapeño g-string makes you a truly Hot Mama for the night. Disassemble your ceiling fan and wear it like a propeller to be Amelia Airhead. Or make yourself into a giant pill, and while carrying a selected Barbie, you can be Valium of the Dolls. Quite simply, any household item can be your theme...a word processor, a food processor (or even a combination of the two — "I can type 50 carrots a minute!").

    The fun ideas never stop, and neither will the party, as each guest arrives wearing more banalities and bric-a-brac than you could find in a Kansas cupboard. Enjoy the food, enjoy the drink, and let's celebrate all the things we aren't!

MINT JEW-LIFT

Ice
½ oz. Spearmint Schnapps
Tea
Lemon or Mint

Fill a tall glass with ice. Add spearmint schnapps and fill remainder of glass with tea. Garnish with lemon or mint.

First concocted by East European immigrants to Mississippi, this drink provides a lift to people of all faiths on a dog-hot afternoon.

STUFFED MUSHROOMS

18 lg. Mushrooms
3 oz. Cream Cheese
2 bsp. Milk
1 lsp. Worcestershire Sauce
¼ cup Water Chestnuts, chopped
2 bsp. Green Onions, chopped
Salt, to taste

Wipe mushrooms and remove stems. Chop stems finely. Mix cheese, milk, and worcestershire sauce until well blended. Add other ingredients and blend. Fill mushroom buttons with mixture and bake on ungreased cookie sheet 12-15 minutes at 350°.

Submitted by Miss Foyer D'Amour

Foyer — that's French for lounge — travels the globe as a Flight Attendress. Who knows in what exotic land she found this stuffed mushroom recipe.

OYSTER-ARTICHOKE SOUP

½ pt. heavy Whipping Cream
1 pt. Half & Half
½ pt. Whole Milk
8 oz. fresh Oysters
1 stick Butter
½ cup all-purpose Flour
5 oz. Carrots, Onions, and Celery, finely chopped
1 8 oz. can Artichokes
1 bsp. White Pepper
1 bsp. Salt
4 bsp. Lemon Juice

Combine whipping cream, half & half, and whole milk in saucepan over medium heat. Do not boil. Add liquid from the oysters to the mixture. Whip vigorously. In a second saucepan, simmer butter and flour for 20 minutes or until browned. Set roux aside for five minutes. Add vegetable mixture and simmer until tender. Fold in oysters and artichokes. Cook an additional three minutes. Combine both mixtures into large saucepan. Season with remaining ingredients to taste. Cook covered on low heat for 30-40 minutes.

Submitted by Miss Shudda Slapta

HAM LOAF SURPRISE

1 lb. ground Smoked Ham
1 lb. ground Pork
2 Eggs, beaten
2 cups Rice Krispies
1 cup Milk
1 lsp. dry Mustard
Black Pepper
1 sm. can sliced Pineapple
¾ cup Brown Sugar
2 bsp. Vinegar
2 lsp. prepared Mustard
2 bsp. Water
your favorite antidepressant

Mix ham, pork, eggs, Krispies, milk, dry mustard, and pepper together and place in a loaf pan. Decorate with pineapple and bake at 350° for 1-1½ hours.

Cook sugar, vinegar, prepared mustard, and water until thickened and baste the loaf as it bakes.

While it's baking, pop the antidepressants according to recommended dosage to help you cope with guests' reactions to being served ham loaf containing Rice Krispies.

Submitted by Miss Bambi Du Feu

This recipe, which was given to Bambi by her late mother, is a must-try. Your company will remember you for being different and original.

NIGHT OUT CASSEROLE

1 package Kraft Macaroni and Cheese

6 Smoky Link Sausages

1 package frozen Peas, thawed

Prepare macaroni and cheese as indicated on box. While it's cooking, apply make-up, gown, and wig.

Pour into a glass casserole dish (glass makes it look nicer!) with sausage links on top in a neat pattern. Wipe yucky smell from fingers. Apply press-on nails and hose.

Put peas over sausages in casserole. Place casserole dish into oven at low cooking temperature for three hours. Go out and have a ball. You'll be ravenous when you get home!

Submitted by Miss Hellen Highwater

Sounds like old party gal Hellen has a great evening out planned in a few easy steps. Watch out, she's off to Camden for the night.

LITTLE JACK HORNER CAKE

1 cup Oil, preferably Wesson

2 cups Sugar

4 Eggs

2 cups self-rising Flour

1 tsp. ground Cloves

1 tsp. Cinnamon

2 sm. jars baby food Strained Plums

1 cup Pecans, chopped

¼ cup Confectioner's Sugar

3 tbsp. dry Sherry

Blend the oil and sugar. Add the eggs one at a time, then add sifted dry ingredients, followed by plums and nuts.

Bake in a greased and floured bundt pan at 350° for 50-60 minutes.

Mix confectioner's sugar with dry sherry until consistency is a thin white sauce. Top cake with sauce.

Submitted by Miss Bonnie Bliss

I had to recite the entire Jack Horner poem a couple of times in my head before I got the gist of this dish's name. Bonnie Bliss, appropriately enough, comes from the Sunshine State and is a busy paralegal when not in drag uniform.

Photo by Lauri Flaquer

GARBO TALKS

½ part Rye Whiskey
¼ part Grapefruit Juice
¼ part Honey, slightly warm for consistency
Cracked Ice

Mix whiskey, grapefruit juice, and honey. Shake well with cracked ice and strain into cocktail glasses.

An afternoon of these and you'll be telling all your secrets.

AN EVENING OF TRANSVESTITE CHANNELING

Props you'll need: crystal ball, burning candles, fun gypsy garb, very light table.

What to do: Find a designated Medium amongst the crowd — this should be simple since most of you are likely extra-larges. Have her close her eyes and imagine she's at a Republican fundraiser. This will put her in a trance-state in no time at all.

Everyone else should join paws and remain very, very quiet. No table titters or gurgling tum-tums allowed! As the spirits appear you may each take turns asking questions.

If a spirit appears who isn't fun, glamourous, or famous enough for your group, you may "channel surf" until a desirable spirit is found.

What a grand way to spend a bad hair night — dim lights and lots of shawls for everyone. Bring on the spirits — how about a former first lady! As your otherworldly evening continues, be sure you've made plenty of food, because you just never know who may appear!

REAL OLD RECIPE FOR COLD BUTTERMILK SOUP

2 good Eggs

4 bsp. Sugar

I Lemon, juice only

I lsp. Vanilla Extract

4 cups Buttermilk

In the soup serving bowl, beat the eggs soundly with sugar, lemon juice, and vanilla. Beat the buttermilk separately and fold in gently.

This simple summer soup is best if served chilled with vanilla cookies or gingersnaps on top. Whipped cream and/or sweetened fruit are also delicious with it.

Submitted by Miss Virginia Ratzasz

Virginia is from Pittsburgh Polska stock. She insists that this family recipe is as simple and satisfying as her first husband, and that it keeps much better than he did.

CRAWFISH NORMA GENE

4 Green Onions, minced

2 ribs de-stringed Celery, minced

I stick Butter

I lb. Crawfish Tails, drained

2 bsp. Flour

2 bsp. melted Butter

I cup Whipping Cream

¼ cup Catsup

4 oz. can Mushroom Stems and Pieces, drained and minced

Salt, Pepper, Worcestershire Sauce, and Tabasco, to taste

3 cup Cognac (optional)

In a small pot, sauté onions, celery, and one stick butter. Add crawfish tails and cook five to ten minutes. Set aside.

In a large pot, make a cream sauce with 2 bsp. flour and 2 bsp. butter. Stir until blended. Add whipping cream and catsup. Boil until thick and add mushroom stems and pieces. Season with salt, pepper, worcestershire, and Tabasco.

Add the crawfish mixture to the cream sauce along with, if desired, the cognac.

Divide into ramekins (small size if using for appetizer; large if for entrée) and heat in 350° oven for 15 to 20 minutes.

Submitted by Miss Giselle Byte

Adds Giselle: "This dish closely resembles the dish served at famous eating establishments. Shrimp or crabmeat may be substituted for the crawfish."

LADY FINGER STEAKS

I Steak, Round or Sirloin

½ cup Flour

½ lsp. Soda

½ lsp. Salt

½ lsp. Pepper

½ lsp. Garlic Salt

½ lsp. Oil

I Egg

½ cup Milk

Cut the steak round or sirloin into 1" pieces. Mix everything else into a batter.

Dip steak into the batter and fry in a bit of oil.

Submitted by Miss Mary Exmass

A great hors d' oeuvres, says Mary. She usually chops an olive in half lengthways to make fingernails to place on the tips of the fingers, then places them in a fan design on a round serving platter alternating them with celery and Cheesewhiz sticks. She's so gifted, that Mary Exmass, and I think this brilliant contribution should exonerate her from any further local humor about coming but once a year.

CHICKEN 'N WINE DISH FOR THE GIRLS

8-10 Chicken Breasts, boned and skinned

Flour

1 Egg, beaten

Italian Bread Crumbs

sm. amount of Oil

1 cube Butter, melted

½ cup red Wine

Non-stick Cooking Spray

Dip chicken breasts in flour and pat dry between hands over newspaper or garbage can. Leave thin layer of flour on chicken. Dip in egg and then in bread crumbs and coat well. Fry in small amount of oil in skillet until light brown (doesn't take long) on both sides.

Mix butter with wine. Spray baking pan with cooking spray. Layer chicken in pan, basting each piece with butter/wine sauce. Cover with foil, sealing edges. You can prepare to this point and refrigerate for use next day.

Bake in 350° over for one hour. Leave covered until ready to serve.

Submitted by Miss Violet Violation, a.k.a. Beaulah "Boom Boom" Bossetti

Miss Violet describes this delicious recipe as, "A special treat for that special night!" Thanks, Boom Boom.

ITALIAN DREAM

½ lb. fresh Porcini (or other) sliced Mushrooms

¼ lb. Prosciutto, chopped

3 bsp. unsalted Butter

½ cup Brandy

1 cup Heavy Cream

⅓ cup fresh (or thawed) Frozen Peas

Salt and Pepper, to taste

½ lb. Egg Noodles

½ lb. Spinach Noodles

¼ cup Parmesan Cheese, freshly grated

Cook the porcini and the prosciutto with the butter in a skillet for six to eight minutes on medium heat. Add the brandy once the mushrooms are wilted. Scrape up any brown bits. Boil the mixture until nearly all liquid is evaporated.

Stir in the cream, peas, salt, and pepper. Simmer while stirring five to six minutes, or until sauce thickens slightly.

While the sauce is cooking, boil the pasta in a kettle of salted water until it is al dente. Drain.

In a bowl toss the pasta with the sauce and the parmesan.

Submitted by Miss Porna May

Doesn't resemble any Italian dreams I've ever met, I mean had, I mean, oh, never mind, but I'll bet this tasty concoction might help you meet one. Thanks, P.M.!

EGGS BENEDICT

4 English Muffins, halved

6 bsp. Butter

8 slices cooked Ham

8 Eggs

3 bsp. Watercress, chopped

Place english muffins on serving plate with a pat of butter and ham slice atop each muffin. In a boiling skillet of salted water, gently break egg — it is easiest to break egg into a cup, and slide egg into water. Turn off heat, cover, and cook three to five minutes. Using a slotted spoon, remove each egg and place onto ham slice. Spoon on Hollandaise sauce. Garnish with watercress.

HOLLANDAISE SAUCE

4 Egg Yolks

½ lsp. Salt

I wtf. Cayenne

I cup Butter, melted

2 bsp. Lemon Juice

Beat egg yolks with electric mixer until thick. Add salt and cayenne. Mix lemon with butter and add to yolk mixture, one bigspoon-at-a-time, beating constantly. SERVE IMMEDIATELY.

Submitted by Miss Goddess Grate

If the truth be told, Miss Grate is good, even great, chums with Miss Goode (remember her?). They often compete in every activity. I've even received competing Hollandaise sauce contributions. Cast your vote for the better of the two.

BOOM-BOOM COOKIES

I cup packed Brown Sugar

½ cup Shortening

I Egg

I lsp. Vanilla

½ lsp. Almond Extract

I oz. unsweetened Chocolate, melted

I cup all-purpose Flour

½ lsp. Baking Soda

½ lsp. Salt

I cup Rolled Oats

½ cup Nuts, chopped

Mix brown sugar, shortening, egg, vanilla, and almond extract in large bowl. Stir in chocolate. Combine flour, baking soda, and salt, and stir into chocolate mixture.

Stir in oats and nuts. Make into a roll about 1½" in diameter. Wrap in waxed paper and refrigerate about four hours or until chilled.

Cut roll into ¼" slices, using a very sharp knife. Place slices about an inch apart on ungreased cookie sheets.

Bake 10-12 minutes at 350°. Makes four dozen.

Submitted by Miss Toya

Miss Toya told me that she remembers eating these cookies as a kid. Her mom would serve them to her and her friends after school, along with big tall glasses of cold Bourbon.

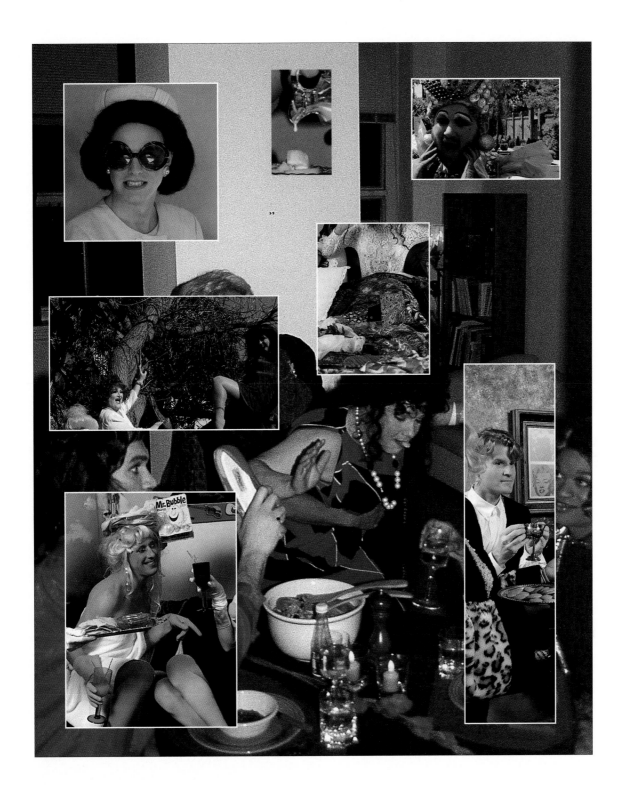

LEFTOVERS

Well, girls, we tried to cram our recipes into the ten novel meal themes provided, but you can only cram so much stuffing into a brassiere before the lace shrieks! What follows are foodstuffs so sumptuous and succulent we just had to donate a little extra bit of space to their presence.

Peruse them with an open mind (which Honey needs to make clear is not the same thing as an airhead) and you will learn to love them all as I have.

SHRIMP DIP

2 cups Shrimp
8 oz. Cream Cheese
¼ cup French Dressing
4 bsp. Mayonnaaise
Salt and Pepper
Red Pepper
Garlic Salt
Onion Salt

Mash shrimp. Add to softened cream cheese. Add other ingredients and spices to taste. Make a day ahead and chill for a better flavor.

Submitted by Miss Violet Violation, a.k.a. Beulah "Boom Boom" Bossetti

HUEVOS RANCHEROS

1 lg. Onion, chopped
Bacon Fat
2 ribs Celery, chopped
1 Bell Pepper, chopped
2 cloves Garlic, chopped
½ lb. Velveeta Cheese
1 can Tomatoes
1 Jalapeño Pepper, diced
1 Pimiento, diced
1 stick Butter
2 cups Ham, cubed
2 doz. Eggs
1 cup Milk
Salt and Pepper, to taste
2 cans Chili without beans, heated

In skillet, sauté onion in bacon fat until clear and limp. Add celery, bell pepper, and garlic. Continue cooking slowly until all are cooked and limp. Set aside and keep warm. While onion is cooking, melt cheese in top of double boiler. Add tomatoes, mashing with spoon until well mixed. Add jalapeño pepper and pimiento. Cook until thoroughly heated. In large skillet, melt butter and cook ham until slightly browned. Add eggs, which have been beaten with milk, salt, and pepper. When eggs are partially set, add sautéed ingredients. Just before eggs are done, stir in cheese mixture. Pour heated chili over eggs to serve.

Submitted by Miss Girtha Goodnight

LUCKY CHENG'S CHINESE LAQUERED DUCK A LA PALOMA

2 2½ lb. Long Island Ducklings
1 cup Soy Sauce
1 cup Honey
¼ cup Rice Vinegar
¼ cup Sesame Oil
¼ cup Water
juice of 6 Louisiana Satsumas or Oranges
2 bsp. Cornstarch, diluted in ¼ cup Water.

Preheat oven to 350°. Place ducks in roasting pan. Mix soy sauce, honey, rice vinegar, sesame oil, and water in a bowl, and pour over ducks. Bake for one hour. Reduce heat to 300°. Bake for one additional hour. Turn ducks every half hour for entire baking period.

SAUCE: Heat juice of satsumas or oranges in skillet until reduced by half. Drain liquid from bottom of roasting pan and add to the juice. Simmer for 20 minutes, then thicken with diluted cornstarch. Simmer an additional ten minutes.

TO SERVE: Debone the ducks. Reheat in 350° oven for 10 minutes. Pour sauce over ducks and serve with stir fry vegetables and steamed jasmine rice.

Submitted by Miss Paloma

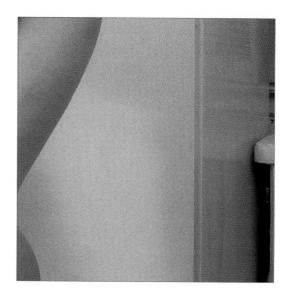

POACHED EGGS OVER CRABCAKES WITH WHITE SAUCE

5 Green Onions, finely chopped
4 Celery Stalks, finely chopped
3 bsp. cooking Oil
¼ lsp. ground Nutmeg
¼ lsp. Thyme
pinch All-spice
pinch ground Cloves
wtf. Tabasco
Salt and Pepper, to taste
1 cup Bread Crumbs
1 10½ oz. can Beef Consommé
1 lb. fresh Lump Crabmeat
2 hard-cooked Eggs, finely chopped
1 bsp. Cornstarch
Flour
½ stick Butter

Sauté the onions and celery in hot cooking oil. As these sauté, add the nutmeg, thyme, all-spice, cloves, Tabasco, salt, and pepper, stirring constantly. Moisten the bread crumbs with part of the consommé and add to the seasoned vegetables. Mix well. Lower the heat. Add crabmeat, chopped eggs, and cornstarch. Stir well.

Make into crab patties, approximately 1½" in diameter and ¾" thick, coating each patty with flour. Add the butter to the cooking oil and re-heat. Fry each patty until brown and crisp.

WHITE SAUCE

2 bsp. Butter
2 bsp. Flour
¾ cup Milk
1 wtf. Tabasco
½ lsp. Nutmeg, freshly ground
½ lsp. Salt
½ cup Gruyère or Swiss cheese, shredded

Melt butter in a heavy saucepan. Slowly add flour, stirring constantly. When thoroughly blended, stir in milk and allow to cook slowly. Add Tabasco, nutmeg, salt, and cheese. Cook slowly until cheese is melted.

Submitted by Miss Isadora Jarr

I hope all you gals know how to poach an egg!

SHRIMP REMOULADE

4 cloves Garlic, minced
1 med. Sweet Pickle, minced
⅔ cup Celery Heart, minced
2 bsp. Catsup
8 bsp. Brown Mustard
1 bsp. Paprika
1 wtf. Cayenne pepper
4 bsp. Horseradish
⅓ cup Green Onion, minced
¼ cup Parsley, minced
½ cup Rice Wine Vinegar
1 cup Salad Oil
¼ lsp. Tabasco
2 lbs. lg. Shrimp, peeled and boiled
one head Lettuce, shredded

Blend all ingredients (except shrimp and lettuce) and mix well. Add boiled shrimp and allow to marinate for about 12 hours. Serve over lettuce.

Submitted by Miss Pottie Chere

SOCK-IT-TO-ME CAKE

1 package Butter Cake Mix
2 sm. Vanilla Pudding Mixes
2 packages Cream Cheese
1 lg. size Whipped Topping
1 lg. can crushed Pineapple
1 lg. can Cherry Pie Filling
1 lg. can Blueberries
1 cup Pecans, chopped

Bake cake per box directions. Let cool. Make vanilla pudding per directions. Mix together cream cheese, pudding, and half of whipped topping.

When cake cools, break up into pieces. Into a large, deep bowl layer cake pieces, pineapple, cherries, blueberries, pecans, and top with layer of pudding mixture. Repeat until all ingredients are used. Top with whipped topping and pecans. Serve from bowl with large serving spoon... enjoy!

Submitted by Miss Shapin Thang

meal

index

Entrées

Side Dishes

Eggs

Desserts

word menagerie for the drag impaired

(glossary)

bejeenies bubbly essence // good sense // wits

B.C. Before Chanel // murky, unimportant, olden days

BM 1. born male 2. big mess 3. biologically mismatched 4. boxed mammaries

co-ho-nes (fr. Spanish) anatomical do-dads

D.Q. 1. Drag Queen, a Miss Nomer for an agile, graceful, glamorous thing gliding around in heels 2. Dairy Queen, a T.V. whose brassiere no longer contains yesterday's news

faboo 1. a metallic version of your favorite hue 2. any party in your honor

fa-cha (fr. Italian) the center of your universe

fag bundle of enjoyment which lights up readily and really smokes

gladrags factor/glitter element categories for measuring drag effectiveness

hoo-ha(s) drag wanna-be(s) in trousers

icky 1. 1970's fashions 2. unplanned body functions 3. beige

nonstandard ladies' accessories e.g. hip pads, oversized gloves, and chain-link wigs

RG 1. real gal 2. matching chromosomes

schmatte (fr. Yiddish) what we stuff ourselves into, and often what we stuff into that

schtick (fr. Yiddish) your behavior and chat whenever outside your trailer

sistren polite plural of bitches

tchotchkied-up (fr. Yiddish) dolled-up // over-assembled

"The Act" ultimate pay-off for all this

titter a glamorous girl-giggle

toidy a pretty name for a filling station

trinkets and **do-dads** and **baubles** distractions from what you are contending with

T.V. Transvestite // girl of the cloth

vixens nice collective name for gals who are no competition at all

vomit-esque icky on someone else

WALTER THOMSON is a freelance commercial and editorial photographer based in New York City. After approximately ten years as a professional musician, his deep interest in photography led him to a career change. Following a period as a photographer's assistant, and shooting a great deal of independent work, one of his first assignments came from costume designer Wendy Stuart, shooting her creations in a makeshift studio.

Since then his work has appeared on CD covers, in magazines, and in catalog illustrations, as well as a series of portraits exhibited at The Alfred Lowenherz Gallery in New York. Recently, he worked as still photographer on location for the short-film, *DOT*, and hopes to pursue more work in the field of movies. Although he is most comfortable behind the camera, he is sometimes asked to print work by other photographers. Some of these photographs have appeared as part of a TV animation, and most recently on a PBS Special.

KERRI McCAFFETY is a professional photographer living in New Orleans. She earned a degree in anthropology at Tulane University, concentrating on ethnographic documentary. For ten years McCaffety has photographed the Crescent City's unique texture and spirit, so it seems inevitable that her career would lead her lens to the colorful culture of Drag Queens.

She has on occasion created photographs that do not contain any men in high heels. McCaffety's award-winning fine art photography, represented by Carol Robinson Gallery in New Orleans, was recently compared to dramatic work of the early photo-romantics Steichen and Imogen Cunningham.

McCaffety's street scenes and Mardi Gras images have been published as post card collections called *New Orleans Street* and *Prints of Vice*. Her work appears in *Allure*, *Historic Traveler Magazine*, *Tribe Magazine*, *Anglo-American Spotlight*, *New Orleans Magazine*, *Rhythm Music Magazine*, *The New Orleans Times-Picayune*, and *OffBeat Magazine*.

LAURI FLAQUER, after many years as a make-up artist in salons and the film, video, and television industry, and after spending the past few years as a photographer, has finally achieved a culmination of her varied experience. Beautifying society women who were private clients was as close as Lauri had come to "drag artistry," but a new level of creative challenge was definitely presented to her with this project, as she made-up many of our "made-up maidens." In addition, working behind the camera allowed her to further develop her other chief professional interest.

Lauri insists she believed in this project from its inception. She felt there would be fascinating people and fun people (nothing like a Drag Queen to brighten one's existence!), and she found that every shoot was more interesting than the previous ones. Lauri also contends that the drag transformation is one of the most impressive human phenomena that she has encountered.

These days, when not photographing men dressed like ladies, Lauri operates a greeting card line which can be found in fine stationary/card shops everywhere.

ALISON GOOTEE was born and raised in New Orleans. She graduated from Louisiana State University with a Bachelor of Fine Arts in Graphic Design and a strong interest in photography.

Since graduating, she has photographed throughout Italy and Spain. Her work has appeared in the film magazine *Cast & Crew*, and she has instructed special ed students in Jefferson Parish's "Very Special Arts Week." She is currently working in New Orleans as a commercial photographer, as well as continuing her art photography.

MISS PORCELANA BISQUE is a graduate of the Cabrini Day School, where she received her degree in laundry scrubbing with a speciality in girdle stain removal, and was a member of the Gentilly Chili Cotillion where she was "Deb Chilian." She currently provides services at Milan's Yugoslav Club, where she is laundress/tendress by day and night. After several attempts at the local and national beauty pageant circuits, where she was tossed off runways by other contestants, she finally found peace and happiness in someone else's dirty laundry, where her hard earned education finally paid off!

MISS CHARITY CASE comes to us from Chalmette by-way-of the New Orleans' Mission. Her whereabouts before and since are unknown.

MISS VERA CHARLES has been entertaining in the Pennsylvania Tri-State area for the past five years. Recent credits include *The Monica Rey Drag Attack* and *The Tinsel Garland Show*. She would like to thank her parents, Faye and Richard, and her drag-mothers Berrie Lyndon, Ineta Shave, Ricky Paris, and the late Danee' Russo for all their support.

MISS SUMMER CLEARANCE has the style of a typical suburban socialite. Somehow she manages to shop all the department store clearance sales in between the luncheons, teas, and charity events with the ladies. Summer's shopping expeditions have left her armoire bursting with black pieces, her signature color. As her mother always says: "Black picks up everything but men and money." She could be wrong!!!

MISS CORDOBA is not your daddy's Oldsmobile. She can take you 0-69 in 4 seconds flat. Cordoba may be an all luxury lady, but there is nothing like a blue collar man to get her all fired up. You can usually find Cordoba cruisin' around New York City with her girlfriends, Caprice and Crown Victoria.

MISS SOFONDA COX was born in a barn in New Mexico. Her mother was very proud of her as she performed mini "shows" for the family as a child. It was not an uncommon occurrence to find her napping with her mother's beehive cover wrapped around her head. She got involved in performing at private parties and did some celebrity appearances while in college. However, this is her first public appearance in over ten years (we know she looks a lot younger than she is). Sofonda's dear mother, Thelma Jo Cox, has a recipe included in this collection.

MISS PHYLLIS DENMARK (a.k.a Randy Patterson) is a New Orleans favorite. Best known for High Camp and her Mardi Gras antics, Phyllis is a past Mardi Gras Queen of Petronius, the oldest Gay carnival organization. Known for her theater work in *Vampire Lesbians of Sodom* and *The High Heeled Women*, Phyllis can also be see in the documentary *Cutting Loose*, which was featured at the 1996 Sundance Film Festival.

MISS MARGERIE DUNNE' grew up in an old plantation in the south, and for her, attending parties and wearing fabulous clothes started early. Now living in New York City, she has continued those values. If not at indoor Bar-B-Ques, she's at fab cocktail parties over looking the city, having fun. It's a full-time job, but someone has to do it.

MISS LYNNE GAYE was born and reared in New Orleans. Her name was bestowed upon her by friends who thought that when she dressed in drag, she was a dead ringer for a local news anchor. When she is not selling china and crystal for a major department store, she enjoys playing volleyball and roller-blading. She has also performed in local gay Mardi Gras balls for the past six years.

LAWRENCE GOBBLE has known Honey van Campe for several years and would do practically anything for his dear friend...thus his appearance in this book.

MISS HELLEN HIGHWATER (known simply as "Hell" to close associates) reigns from beautiful South Central Los Angeles. An avid wrestler, Hellen also enjoys fly fishing, kick-boxing, nude sunbathing, and entering High-Hair contests. One of Hellen's favorite pastimes is watching old *Baretta* and *Dinah Shore* reruns, and she NEVER misses an episode of *The Price is Right*. Hellen puts away about a fifth of Jack and three packs of Pall Malls a day and is currently employed in a bath house in Detroit.

WESS HUGHES (a.k.a. Miss Sucha Delite) is a New Orleans actor who has appeared in over 200 plays and musicals. He is a member of the Krewe of Petronius, a New Orleans Mardi Gras organization. Wess is currently reigning as Queen Petronius XXXV. Costumes are his life!!!

MISS BIANCA JAGGERMEISTER is a fresh face on the New Orleans social scene. She recently completed her schooling at the Fabiana LaBeouf School for Wayward Girls. Her busy social calendar is filled with Elks Lodge Meetings, high school prom blind dates, and as the primary lap dancer for the local Teamsters #401. She is also available for weddings and bar mitzvahs. Her long term goals include: turning 21, raising sheep, and getting her pilot's license.

MISS SARAH C. JAMES was born flawless and, consequently, was drafted into the Miss Gay Galaxy beauty circuit where she won every contest lying down. Later, she was appointed Drag Queen Laureate of the U.S., Mexico, and Pago Pago. Her hobbies include sewing, watching Walt Disney movies, and rubbing up against prickly pears.

models

MISS JEM JENDER says, "When your home state's motto is *Live Free or Die*, even the most obtuse can understand how a young boy can make the transition from the lead role in *OLIVER!* to a career as a prima ballerina, and can now be America's Sweetheart and Queen of Dragdom." At the tender young age of 12, after a childhood career in musical theater, Jem received a full scholarship to train in classical ballet. Jem has danced and studied with The Boston Ballet, The Joffrey, The Pennsylvania Ballet, Chataugua Dance Theater, and The Universal Ballet of Korea. In 1987, Jem signed with Ballet Trockadero De Monte Carlo, and a drag ballerina was born. She has done guest interviews on *Entertainment Tonight*, *The Jon Stewart Show*, *Hard Copy*, *Howard Stern*, *MTV's House of Style*, *VH-1's Fashion Television*, *Late Night With Conan O'Brien*, and *Saturday Night Live*. Jem has also modeled for designers Donna Karan, Armani, and Isaac Mizrahi, to name a few. Jem has also written *33rd and 3rd*, her very own screenplay which is currently in development. She also writes a weekly column for *WIRE-NEW YORK*.

MYSTERY MAN, located somewhere in the French Quarter, he can often be seen walking briskly.

MISS ETA MANN is proud to be counted as one of Honey's friends. Living in the suburbs, Eta has found Honey's compilation of recipes invaluable, because, in Eta's words, "Cooking is a Drag." Eta doesn't wear women's clothes too often. Mostly when she goes out to dinner.

MISS NAPPI MERKIN is new to the drageuse arena (in a manner of speaking). Nappi has recently received fashion accolades for reintroduction of the perruque de Venus, occasioned by her creative dissection of an old Kalinsky fur. Go get 'em, Miss M!

MISS VARLA JEAN MERMAN, who claims to be the illegitimate daughter of Ethel Merman and Ernest Borgnine, grew up in the hot, steamy city of New Orleans, where she is the perennial hostess of New Orleans' Annual Bourbon Street Awards. Her short films have been the topic of a film festival and forum at Arizona State University. In 1994, Ms. Merman moved to New York. In 1995, she wrote and starred in *Varla and the Man Who Got Away*, a one-woman show produced by Susanne Bartsch and Dewar's, which was named one of the five best productions of 1995 by *HX Magazine*. Ms. Merman has been the opening act for John Epperson, a.k.a. Lypinska. In January, 1996, Ms. Merman completed a six-month run at Eighty Eight's of *Merman•Shanz!*, her weekly variety show. Varla Jean's vocal performance has been reviewed in numerous magazines such as *New York Magazine*, *The Daily News,* and *The Village Voice. Time Out* has referred to her as "the outrageously brilliant drag diva" who can pull off "some rather astounding vocal feats."

models

COUNTESS MONESTAT THE 7TH

was once told by a wise friend, "If you can't be spectacular...make a spectacle!" And so it is with this sense of style and sense of humor that she takes part in "entertaining," if it merits such terminology. Her entertaining is not only for the audience and her fans, but for the soul. It's just one of the many activities she takes part in which makes up her definition of "celebrating life!"

MISS JACKIE O'MAGAAD, having

made numerous appearances as the former First Lady prior to her untimely transition from V.I.P to R.I.P, conveniently sprouted wings in the late Spring of 1994. Since that time there have been Jackie sightings all across the country on High Holy Days: Halloween in San Francisco, Carnival in Provincetown, Southern Decadence in New Orleans. Where will she appear next?

MISS PLEASURE O'RIELLEY offers

this advice to her many fans: "After a long hard week of cocktail parties, shopping, man-hunting, not to mention work, remember to always set aside one day a week devoted to you, and only to you. A day of beauty, if you will, or as I call it, a day of Pleasure. Exfoliate, bubble bath, skin toner, the whole nine inches, oh, I mean yards. And never forget to moisturize. Hey, I love the nite-life and like to boogie as much as the next girl, but always remember to be true to yourself and pamper a little. Play safe, love hard, and don't forget to pluck those eyebrows."

MISS MAXINE PADD In the words of

this Barbie of Burlesque, Star of Stage and Screen, "It's not only that the pictures got bigger...so did I!" The former Miss I.G.B.A.B.E. (the International Gay Bowling Organization's Beauty Queen) of 1993 explodes: "I'm beautiful, dammit! They really like me...really they do!"

DADDY WARPED POCKETS is a

star of stage and screen, and Bud Light commercials, who's lust for Varla Jean remains true and firm.

MISS TINGLY PULLMAN comes from

a privileged background, being an heiress of the famed Pullman car lineage. A former international forearm model, Tingly recently retired to devote her energies to social causes such as "Drags against Drugs" and her own "Prison Wig Outreach Program."

MISS IVANA B. QUEEN lists her vital

statistics as: Sign: Libra; Height: 6'3"; Weight: 195 lbs; Bust: 48"; Waist: 34"; Hips: 45". Her turn-ons are: Electrical Appliances, Fruit Headresses, and Royal Weddings. Her turn-offs are: Republicans, Shaving, and Nuclear Powerplants. Ivana describes her ideal man as, "Rich, Powerful, Corruptable" and her life's ambition is, "To rule my man...my kingdom...my world!"

models

MISS SELIPHANE RAPPA (a.k.a Greg

Prosser), being of pseudo-sound mind and rock-hard manly body does soundly swear that she did outfit her musculature in a fabulous red flapper and shabby borrowed wig on her 29th birthday (she wouldn't lie!) for her very good friend and ex-roommate, Miss Honey van Campe. Honey, only for you. You are the mostest!

MISS MONICA REY has one of

America's most impressive Drag resumes' with top pageant honors ranging from Miss Portland, Oregon (1981) to Imperial Princess Royale – Reno, Nevada (1985). Her Mistress of Ceremonies engagements are quite numerous and our Lady of Glamour is no stranger to pageant judging. Currently, she performs in the Pennsylvania/ New Jersey vicinity: Come see Monica's *Drag Search* at The Cartwheel (New Hope, Pennsylvania) on Mondays and *The Monica Rey Drag Attack* at the Colosseum (Sayreville, New Jersey) every Tuesday.

MISS RONDA-LAY is originally from

Cheeseland. Someday she hopes to return. Until then, Ronda-Lay makes her living in New York City as Finance Director of a Fortune 500 company – unfortunately not in the dairy industry. For fun she enjoys a nice cheddar while having some "good clean fun" with Mr. Bubble (and his friends).

MISS DELICROIX ST. JOHN hails

from the back waters of Louisiana's Bayou Country – Delicroix Island. As a baby, she was suckled in a crab trap by her Maw-Maw and was fed a diet of oysters and nutria, which predicted her diva-like looks. Growing up in a small cajun fishing community, she learned early how to bait a hook and reel 'em in. Presently, Ms. St. John uses these skills as she drags the murky gutters of the French Quarter looking for seafood and manages the Women's Foundations counter at Krauss.

GEORGE ANTHONY SARGIA is an

Actor of both Stage and Television. He has appeared in Comedies, Dramas, and Musicals, and his roles have included Reverend Crisparkle in *Mystery of Edwin Drood*, Beverly Carlson in *Man Who Came to Dinner*, Renfield in *Dracula*, Sir Andrew Aguecheek in Shakespeare's *Twelfth Night*, the singing Waiter in *She Loves Me*, and Baron Von Swieton in *Amadeus*.

MISS BRENDA STARR (a.k.a. Robert

Tabor) landed on this planet in New York City sometime in her 20s. As a costume she has developed a unique and humorous drag style which brings many wonderful opportunities, and makes her as happy as all her imaginary boyfriends. Life is really good...!

MISS RONDA DEL STEAM is at first

glance an unlikely victim for this publication since her background includes an Ohio upbringing and many years working at the K-Mart. Fortunately, Ronda came to see the light, has altered her ways, and now, more than ever before, has truly come to view life as the Drag that is should be.

MISS TOOKIE was born seven years ago on the balcony of a French Quarter bar. Since her birth, she knew she was a star. She has been performing for the past three years. Entertaining at benefit shows and major Mardi Gras balls is what keeps her busy in the world of drag. She loves to design all of her own costumes and gowns, and thanks to her husband, their creations come to life. And that's what makes Miss Tookie feel real!

MISS TIFFANY TUCKER was born in the good ole' South. Not much happened to her — but then she was named Queen Polyphemus the VII! After this crowning achievement, she began performing for charity events and in plays. Her career has continued successfully, and many consider her the greatest performer of her time!

MISS CLAIRE A. VUOYANT is a poetess and vegetarian who would rather go naked than wear fur, but agreed to don dead animal skin as part of her drag outfit one time, and one time only, for her new found friend, Honey van Campe.

MISS VIOLET VIOLATION (a.k.a Beulah "Boom Boom" Bossetti) is a novice in the Drag world. Her first "drag" appearance occurred when she was asked by friends to emcee the "High Hair Contest" during Southern Decadence in New Orleans at Good Friends Bar in 1994. She has since repeated that honor and is looking forward to doing so again. As "Boom Boom" Bossetti, she was the first runner up in the first official "Miss Trailer Trash Contest" at Good Friends. She can be seen only twice a year, once on Mardi Gras day, and again during Southern Decadence.

VULVINA AND STARINA, the Goddesses from Venus, are skipping across the galaxy on a mission to seek alternative hangouts inhabited by other compatible beings. Incognito, both goddesses frequent Dallas, Texas, USA, Earth, where they dress daily as earthlings. While here, Vulvina's alias is Bill Ory, and she works as a hairstylist. Starina is known as L.B. Rosser, and she is a hair and make-up artist. They are enjoying their visit!

MISS STEPHANIE WILLIAMS (a.k.a. Patrick Brewer) is an entertainer who has worked throughout the United States. She has been a cast member in many of the top clubs in the country, and has a long list of accomplishments in the art of female impersonation, and has won many competitions in female impersonation. Stephanie has also worked in theatrical films and appeared in numerous publications. She has been a featured portrait subject of artist/photographer Judy Cooper. The character illusions created by this entertainer are many. Among the favorites are Marilyn Monroe, Patsy Cline, Dolly Parton, and a host of comedy characters as Passion's Playtoy.

photo

index

THE FUN NEVER ENDS...

Honey's latest bouquet
of wise words
for the air-borne,
sea-going, and
highway-hugging
holidayers!

Adventures While A Broad

The Basics: Picking, Packing, and Posing

🏃

Games, Gowns, and all-around Gal-Groovin'

🏃

State-side story-making and how to introduce some real-international intrigue

🏃

Trunk-loads more!

Coming to a plugged-in purveyor of fun stuff near you!!!

Let's Go Shopping!

Are you pooped from a long day at work? Are you bored with your wardrobe? Are you longing to redecorate? Where better to turn than the retailer that understands your special needs like no boutique in the country? (Plus, think of the agony of squeezing into those pumps for a grueling trip to the mall!)

Get comfy on your couch, pour yourself a glass of chardonnay, and pick up that cellular, girl!

Ask for *Personal Regalia Paraphernalia*, a free catalog and your ticket to a better way of living!

1.888.IDO.DRAG
436.3724

PONTALBA PRESS
4417 Dryades Street • New Orleans, LA 70115
504.899.7970   fax 504.899.6573

Call for a listing of other titles available.